GOD'S FENCES

OF

TRIALS AND TRIUMPHS

PROTECTION AND PROVIDENCE

GRACE AND LOVE

Catherine A. Garrett

All Scripture quotations, unless otherwise indicated, are taken from the HOLY BIBLE, NEW INTERNATIONAL VERSION@, NIV@ 1973, 1978, 1984 by International Bible Society. Used by permission of Zondervan. All rights reserved.

Unless otherwise indicated, all Scripture quotations are taken from the LIVING BIBLE, copyright @ 1971. Used by permission of Tyndale House Publishers, Inc., Carol Stream, Illinois 60188. All rights reserved.

ACKNOWLEDGEMENTS

Thank you, Amanda, for diligently working on the book cover. I also want to thank my family for their support. But above all, I give all glory to Christ my Lord and Savior for this book. I pray that when you read this book, you will be blessed and encouraged by God's fences in your daily life. Also, I'm praying you will realize that everything you experience here on earth is just another chance to grasp how wide, how long, how wide and how deep is the Father's love. I pray also that learning the lesson that God has given you is just another opportunity for you to grow deeper, so that God can mold you into the person who He created you to be.

~~ Trust in the Lord and do good; dwell in the land and enjoy safe pasture. Delight yourself in the Lord and He will give you the desires of your heart.~~
Psalm 37: 3 & 4

CONTENTS

Introduction..................................6

Fences of Security....................16

Mayhem and Miracles............25

Feelings and Faith....................39

Follies and Footsteps..............48

Requirements and resources...................60

Deserts and Rainforests.........74

Death and Life..........................88

My Father's Legacy...............100

Open Fences of Faith and Grace............114

CHAPTER ONE

INTRODUCTION

    I grew up in the heart of Kansas where there is much more grass than there is concrete. I moved to California in December 1979 with my husband, my two young children and one on the way. The more I'm around concrete, the more I miss the fields of Kansas. Even though I have lived and worked in the Golden State for over thirty-nine years, it still doesn't feel like home to me; at least here on this earth. My body may be here in California but my heart is and will always be in Kansas. If a Kansas sports team plays a local California sports team, I always cheer for the Kansas sports team. I grew up in the heart of Kansas but you could also say that Kansas is in my heart. As they say, 'you can take the girl out of the country but you can't take the country out of the girl'. I've chosen to continue to reside here in California because of a good job, my children and grandchildren. Now that two of my three children have moved out of the area, my desire is to retire to the earthly "home" that resides in my heart – Kansas. Whether I make it there or not, I know that God will be with me no matter where I end up.

    Far as the eye can see, there are rolling hills of green pastures in the spring and summer. In late summer there are fields full of hay bales, cornstalks and glowing golden wheat swaying in the wind. Some folks have joked that a person can stand on a rock and see clear across the entire state, but those folks haven't been through the Flint Hills in Northeastern Kansas along Interstate 70. I would imagine even those who thought that the earth was flat, changed their minds when they ventured into those Kansas Flint Hills.

    The farm I grew up on was only forty acres, but to me it felt more like thousands. It was surrounded by fields of brome grass, corn, wheat, alfalfa, soy beans and grazing Holstein cattle. We also had a vegetable garden and several fruit trees, including apple, peach and pear, which I loved eating ripe right off of the tree. This land was farmed by my father and before that, my grandfather. In the early years when my dad was still young, they used a horse-drawn wagon for hauling hay and grain, but as far back as I remember, we used an old John Deer tractor. At top speed it may have only gone as fast as ten miles an hour but was a staple to farming. My dad used the tractor and wagon to haul grain to the grain elevator in town and to pull the hay wagon from the field to the barn. I remember riding in the wagon that was full of wheat while eating granules of wheat along the way to my hometown grain elevator a mile down the road. I wouldn't have imagined years later that I would be wheat intolerant. I also remember spending many hours on the tractor in the field pulling a disc leveling the ground for planting. The engine of that tractor was as loud as a 747 coming in for a landing. I could sing to the top of my lungs and no one could hear me. It was probably a good thing too!

    Growing up on a farm was a lot of hard work but it also gave me a good work ethic, a sense of achievement; as well as a peaceful good feeling. I was very comfortable within those forty acres with no thought of harm inside those fences that bordered it. To me, it was like a sanctuary; a sanctuary of peace and safety. I learned that hard work was rewarding and it developed a strong sense of right and wrong in the way I looked at life and how I treated God's nature and people. We respected the land and God's creatures big and small. But most importantly, we learned to respect ourselves and each other. Growing up in a peaceful Christian home was a blessing; something that I will always cherish.

Looking back to those farm days has brought me lots of fond memories of growing up in the country; its freedom and happiness. Despite the fact that we had no running hot water, had to use an outdoor toilet, gathered wood during the harsh winter months to burn in our wood burning stove, which was our only heating source for the majority of the house, and hang our clothes on a clothesline, I was blessed to have had lived there. Farming was a hard life but it was also a learning experience. If you've lived on a farm you'll understand what I'm talking about. If you haven't, you really missed out. Despite the one hundred degree weather, I learned that if I didn't wear long sleeve shirts when I hauled in the bales of hay from the field, my arms would have looked like I got into a fight with a bear. I also learned not to mess with stinging critters, to ensure that my feet didn't get too close to a hoof of a fifteen hundred pound milk cow, avoid stepping on rusty nails; especially when I'm barefoot, always wear gloves when handling wood so I don't get splinters, remember to go to the bathroom before I put on my snow suit over several layers of winter clothing, and elbow grease isn't found under the sink.

Just like those physical farm fences, God places us within, what I call, His teaching-moment fences of life; even though it may not always be our choice-and it usually isn't. There's duel action involved here – God's providence and human free will. Sometimes His providence leads us into some circumstances that brings about difficulties, resulting in sadness and pain. Other times, He fills us with His rich blessings. But mostly, He brings circumstances into our lives in order to teach us HIS life lesson that He had specifically designed for each of us. This lesson isn't taught during good times but during trials and difficulties. I believe my life lesson He designed for me is "FAITH"; faith in Him regardless of what I see or don't see in front of me and faith in His plan even when I don't understand it. Unfortunately, I have had to learn this lesson over and over and over again through many circumstances of my life. And, I'm still learning this lesson today; even now as I'm writing this.

For me and for other believers, God places fences that are not only for providence but for protection. There were so many instances on the farm, as well as today, where God protected me, like getting caught in a lightning storm while out in an open field, being chased by a swarm of hornets or when severe storms moved through the area. I'm sure you can think of a time when God protected you from harm or even death. Perhaps it was narrowly escaping an auto accident or maybe surviving cancer. God promises in Hebrews 13:6 *"The Lord is my helper, I will not be afraid. What can man do to me?"*

    Most times it's hard to look at our current circumstances to see what God is doing in our lives and what He wants to teach us through those circumstances. I know it is for me. We can't see where our footsteps will lead. We can only see where we've been; like footprints in the sand. Most of the time, I start to rely on my own wisdom and strength instead of God's, which is kind of like walking through the dark with my eyes closed or walking to the outhouse without a flashlight. As a result, I'm not depending on His light to guide me and I easily stumble and lose my way. Abraham had to learn this lesson too.

    In Genesis, God told Abraham that Sarah would have a child; even in their old age. But year after year they waited and got impatient. So they tried to do it all on their own but that wasn't God's choice or plan. Despite their failures, God, in His time, gave them a son named Isaac, who bore Jacob, the father of the twelve tribes of Israel. Despite their futile efforts and my futile efforts, we become impatient with God's timing. God reminds us that He always comes through in His time; not ours, and get us out of the mess we've made. God is always on time; never late or never early. There are many more lessons that Abraham's story could tell us but I will continue that journey in later chapters.

    Until I get to the end of myself, I can't let go and let God work. I'm also a lot like Thomas, a disciple of Jesus. The book of John tells us that Thomas wouldn't believe that Jesus rose from the dead until he saw Jesus' hands, feet and side with his own eyes. Most of the time I have to see to believe too, but Jesus reminded Thomas and even me, that more blessed is the one who believes without seeing.

Throughout my life, I have found that God is my fence of protection and safety. I can't see it with my own eyes like those fences on the farm but the Holy Spirit and His Word tells me they are all around me. In Psalm 34:7, it says *"The angel of the Lord encamps around those who fear Him and He delivers them."* Also, in Psalm 91:4, God promises *"He will cover you with his feathers and under His wings you will find refuge; His faithfulness will be your shield and rampart."*

I also realize that there is a major difference between those farm fences and God's fences. On the farm there were many summer storms which brought damaging winds that knocked some of the fences down or the fences became decayed due to time and age. God's fences, however, will never decay or be torn down by any power on Earth or in Heaven. They are eternal and because of that, I can depend totally on God and His fences now and in the future. I can trust Him and His Word. Psalm 145:13 says *"Your kingdom is an everlasting kingdom, and your dominion endures through all generations. The Lord is faithful to all His promises and loving toward all He has made."*

As I previously mentioned, I have experienced many miss steps, failures, feeling of insecurity in certain situations, disobedient actions, and complacency in my walk with the Lord, and at times, doubting the Lord's direction He was taking me or what He was doing in my life. However, I've also experienced hope, victory, and a willingness to take the path God chose for me and enjoy peace in my journey. I am sure that anyone reading this has had the same experiences in your journey with the Lord; some failures and some victories. No matter what road God takes us down, we all have the assurance that He walks beside us and goes before us; even in death. Although I've always felt like Kansas was my earthly home, my real destination is my Heavenly home. God continues to provide many life-changing lessons to teach us in our journey before we see Him face to face. Whether our journey is one day or one hundred years, His omnipresent fences surround us and transform us into His image and everlasting Glory.

God is the potter, we are the clay. He uses all of life's circumstances, good or bad, to mold us into the likeness of His Son Jesus Christ. God cares more about our character than our comfort. Isaiah 64:8 says *"O Lord, you are our Father, We are the clay, you are the potter; we are all the work of your hand."* It's God's job to mold us and our job to yield; to be willing to learn from Him and to be changed by Him into His image. That life-long process takes faith; faith in God's plan for our lives and believe that *".....in all things God works for the good of those who love Him, who have been called according to His purpose."* Romans 8:28.

I pray that this book will give you some encouragement to continue in your life-long journey with

God and always look for the lesson God wants you to learn. You never know which trial or circumstance God will use as an opportunity to bring you closer to Him and show you that His Grace is all sufficient. To quote the Apostle Paul in II Corinthians 12:9 & 10 *"My Grace is sufficient for you, for my power is made perfect in weakness. Therefore I will boast all the more gladly about my weaknesses, so that Christ's power may rest on me"*. Paul accepted God's fences by putting aside his own weaknesses and trusting in God's strength to finish the race before him.

As God's children, God has pre-ordained a path for us to walk while here on earth. God didn't promise a life free of pain and trials, but He did promise to always be with us through them. During Jesus' last instructions and encouragement to His disciples prior to the cross, he told them (and us) in John 16:33 *"I have told you these things so that in me you may have peace. In this world you will have trouble. But take heart! I have overcome the world."*

Although I've left those farm fences behind and reminisce of the joy they brought me, I now live in God's fences today while continuing to learn the life-long lesson of faith. As I look ahead toward the end of my earthly journey and enter God's Heavenly Eternal Kingdom, I am sure that between now and then, the remainder of my journey will include many more lessons of faith.

God continually reminds me that I only see through the glass dimly, but one day I will see Him face to face and then I will fully understand. In the meantime, I will continue to learn the lesson of faith; to trust Him more and more each day; even in the most difficult circumstances. Some days I will fail. Some days I will succeed. But my hope is in Jesus and I will trust in His promise to never leave me or forsake me. I know that He loves me and no one can snatch me out of his hand. Jesus says in John 10:27-28, *"My sheep listen to my voice; I know them, and they follow me. I give them eternal life, and they shall never perish; no one can snatch them out of my hand. My Father who has given them to me, is greater than all; no one can snatch them out of my Father's hand."* These are the fences we all need to rely on because they are planted in an eternal foundation not made with hands and cannot be moved or destroyed. His fences are like a spiritual road signs, headlights for our path, and a boundary of protection from harm.

  Whether you live on a farm or in the city, look for God's fences. They are all around you; even when you can't see them. God's fences will bring you safety and security that the world can't provide.

- ❖ Fences of truth
- ❖ Fences of hope
- ❖ Fences of protection
- ❖ Fences of providence
- ❖ Fences of miracles
- ❖ Fences of guidance
- ❖ Fences of faith
- ❖ Fences of grace

When we live within God's fences, we will live in peace; a peace that the world cannot give. Jesus said in John 14:27 *"Peace I leave with you; my peace I give you. I do not give to you as the world gives. Do not let your hearts be troubled and do not be afraid."* Trust in God and His fences. Be ready and willing to learn your life lesson in your journey. You just never know where that will lead you and the blessings you will attain.

CHAPTER TWO

FENCES OF SECURITY

(TO WALK ON WATER YOU NEED TO KNOW WHERE THE ROCKS ARE)

Just as my security as a young girl were those fences on the farm, God has been my fence of security throughout my life. You could say that each fence post represented God's promises. The freedom that I felt on the farm has become my example of the freedom I have in Christ. The following are some verses that talk about God's promises of security.

Job 11:18 *"You will be secure, because there is hope; you will look about you and take your rest in safety."*

Psalm 91:5 *"You will not fear the terror of night, nor the arrow that flies by day."*

Psalm 125:1 *"Those who trust in the Lord are like Mount Zion, which cannot be shaken but endures forever."*

Although I felt secure within those fences, I was quite insecure inside, which was reflected outwardly by the feeling of insecurity at school. I was naturally shy and introverted. I was insecure about how I looked, how I was dressed and whether people around me would like me or accept me for who I was. I was also afraid of making a mistake or not living up to someone's expectations. Being teased every day at school certainly didn't help my insecurity, in fact, increased it all the more. It drained me emotionally and I struggled academically. Throughout the school day, I tried to avoid all the other kids and kept to myself. In a sense, I made myself invisible and hoped that no one saw me so I wouldn't be made fun of. I couldn't wait until the school day was finished so I could return to the farm to again feel safe from ridicule and hurt.

When I got hit on the head with a chalk board eraser by a boy in my first grade class, I knew school was not going to be kind to me and it was going be a very long twelve years. Not knowing his intentions, I didn't know if he liked me or hated me. Regardless of that uncertainty, it hurt and I went off crying. It certainly didn't help me get over my insecurity but instead, it only deepened it. When I now look back on the situation, in all likely hood, he was probably trying to hit another male classmate and my head just got in the way. But to me, it didn't matter at the time.

If I would have turned to God in those instances, I could have felt His fences of peace and security that only He could bring during that hurtful and lonely time in my life. God would have reminded me of David's words in Proverbs 29:25, *"Fear of man will prove to be a snare, but whoever trusts in the Lord is kept safe."* Again, I didn't learn that life lesson of having faith & trust in God alone that I was supposed to learn; even at an early age. Instead of having faith in God and feeling peaceful knowing I was loved by Him, I left those school days feeling defeated and abandoned by my peers. Maybe I should have been more like Noah.

Genesis tells about Noah who was a great example of faith, despite the ridicule of those around him. The people that God created had become greatly wicked but God saw that Noah was a righteous man, blameless among the people of his time, walked with God and always conducted his affairs according to God's will. God saw how corrupt the people had become so He told Noah that He was going to destroy the earth with a flood and to build an ark to save him, his family and animals.

Although I'm sure Noah didn't fully understand everything God told him, he began building the ark as God specified. He fully had faith and security in God's word and knew that God's plan would be fulfilled; despite that the people around him started ridiculing him. I suppose that it would make more sense if they were located near a large body of water but it appeared they were not. Although it took him one hundred years to build the ark, Noah exercised faith day after day in the face of impossibility and mockery. He had full faith in a God he didn't even see and because of that, God kept him and his family safe. Through God's direction and Noah's obedience (providence & free will), they entered the ark when Noah was six hundred years old. Noah felt God's fences of security and at peace no matter if all he knew up to that point was being destroyed around him. God rewarded him for his faith; a lesson he needed to learn. Hebrews 11: 7 the 'Hall of Faith', commends Noah for his belief in God's direction despite the world's view around him. *"When he heard God's warning about the future, Noah believed Him even though there was then no sign of a flood, and wasting no time, he built the ark and saved his family. Noah's belief in God was in direct contrast to the sin and disbelief of the rest of the world-which refused to obey-and because of his faith he became one of those whom God has accepted.*" (LB)

 During the time I lived on the farm, my grandparents, who lived in the nearby town, would come out to visit. To me, my grandmother always seemed quite serious but my grandfather had quite a wonderful sense of humor. He wore overalls and would fill his pockets with candy and gum which we were allowed to hunt for. We would search each and every pocket until we found the hidden loot. For my sisters and me, it was like digging for hidden treasure.

 One day while he was visiting, I asked him to help me learn to ride a bike. With my insecurity, learning to ride a bike was like trying to jump over the Grand Canyon on a tricycle. It seemed impossible. But my grandpa reassured me that he would hold onto the back of my bike until I was confident enough to handle it myself without help. I remember telling him "Don't let go grandpa until I'm ready! Don't let go!" He answered with reassurance that he wouldn't. After we tried it a few times, I felt like I got the hang of it but didn't feel secure enough to try it myself without his help. We set off again and again, each time asking him not to let go. Pretty soon I no longer heard him behind me so I looked back and discovered he had already let go a few feet back. I immediately felt my insecurity returning because he no longer had ahold of my bike and I and the bike went tumbling down. After a few more tries, I finally learned to ride it on my own without his help. Even now, I'm still telling my Heavenly Father "Daddy! Don't let go!"

Just like my grandpa had ahold of my bike, God has ahold of my life as well as your life even though we don't always see Him. He knows us, He sees us, and He meets us where we are at and loves us despite of our insecurities. I'm sure when Noah started building a boat out in the middle of nowhere, he at times felt insecure about what God had instructed him to do. God had ahold of Noah, saw his faith and kept him and his family safe until they reached the destination that God had planned for them. Throughout his journey, Noah trusted God's fences of security and providence. His faith in God was stronger than his fear of man or circumstances. Oh, to have faith like Noah!

Another example of putting full trust in the Lord during insecure circumstances is seen in the story of the disciples while sailing in a boat on the lake to Capernaum. It became dark and a strong wind came up causing the waters to grow rough. Since Jesus had not joined them at this point, the disciples began feeling afraid and insecure. After rowing few miles, they saw Jesus approaching the boat walking on the water. This made them even more afraid because they at first didn't recognize them. But then Jesus seeing that they were terrified told them "It is I; don't be afraid." Then, upon Jesus' request to come, Peter stepped out of the boat and started to walk to Jesus. As long as he focused on the Lord, he didn't slip down into the water but when he took his eyes off of Him, he started to sink. Jesus immediately pulled Peter up and they both entered the boat. Then Jesus said to Peter in Matthew 14:31b *"You of little faith, why did you doubt?"* Peter learned through this experience and dependence on God, that God's fences of security was holding him up above the deep lake water.

Like Peter, I've had to learn to look past my weaknesses and depend on God's strength. God has strengthened me through my weaknesses by learning to depend on Him instead of my own strength during those times. When I was young, the time came to get the bales of hay out of the field and into the barn. My dad would pull the wagon filled with hay bales right next to the barn. On the second story there was a loft with a very large barn door through which the bales were placed. My older sister and I would be at the door to receive the bales that my dad pitched up to us, pull them away from the door and stack. I thought my dad was the strongest man in the world. It seemed with very little effort, my dad would heave up those heavy bales from the wagon to the loft. When all but one bale was left on the wagon, he would hoist that one up too. But, despite how strong my dad was, God's strength outweighs his strength or any other man's strength by far. Although I saw my dad as super human, he was weak in comparison to God's strength. Luke 1:37 says *"For nothing is impossible with God."*

Throughout my life, I have gone through many experiences in a weak and insecure state, not even knowing if I had the strength to go on. One of which, was the passing of my husband and father days apart, which I will go into more detail in a later chapter. I had three children to raise on my own and was totally unprepared to deal with this situation. But, as God has promised, I found my strength in Him within His fences of security; even in my insecurity to deal with such an unexpected tragedy. I couldn't have gone through that without Him. I'm sure you have had similar experiences in your life. It could be a death or maybe an illness or another family crisis; perhaps losing a job or even being persecuted for believing in Jesus like Noah was. Paul says in II Corinthians 12:10 *"That is why, for Christ's sake, I delight in weaknesses, in insults, in hardship, in persecutions, in difficulties. For when I am weak, then I am strong."*

    I'm sure all of us have had experiences like Peter. Actually I'll have to admit, I've had way too many. When I take my eyes off of Jesus, I fall. But when I turn and look to Him, He is always right there to pick me up and get me back on the right path. When we fail, He will never allow us to stay where we are because of His great love for us. He does that because He has a very important lesson for us to learn. Our security is in God alone, not man. He is our audience of 'One'. He is the center of everything and when we place Him in the center of our lives, He will keep us centered in Him. In fact, the verse that is the center of the Bible shows us God's truth that everyone should live by. That verse is Psalm 118:8 *"It is better to take refuge in the Lord than to trust in man"*. Both Noah and Peter had to learn that lesson. Despite those words of ridicule which Noah had to endure and Peter's wimpy faith, God rewarded their faith despite their impossible circumstances. When we learn that lesson, we will be secure within His fences, even in the midst of insecure experiences or situations that we encounter in our journey. Psalm 28:7 says *"The Lord is my strength and my shield; my heart trusts in Him, and I am helped."*

God does not promise a care-free life during our time here on Earth but He does promise that He will never leave us or forsake us (Psalm 27:10) and we can rely on Him through each life's circumstance. His Spirit is always present to guide our footsteps so that we grow closer to God and fulfill all that He has planned for us. We just need to trust Him and His fences of security in that journey, but sometimes that's easier said than done. To me and you, seeing is believing but to God, believing is seeing.

On the farm, the fences that surrounded our farm were made of wood, which in time disintegrated and didn't remain forever. Sometimes we build our fences of security using the wrong materials that won't last either such as other people, family, wealth, fame or our own selfish desires. Instead, build on God's fences of security, his Word, His plan and His Providence. These will last forever as God's Word reminds us in Proverbs 14:26 *"He who fears the Lord has a secure fortress, and for his children it will be a refuge."* God's fences are secure and He will be our refuge in times of trouble. The most important element in these fences is that they are eternal fences that nothing or no one can destroy.

True security only comes through our faith in Jesus Christ. That means no matter what happens here on this earth, we know that God's fences of security will never be taken away by anything or anyone. When we trust Him as our firm foundation we will be secure now and forever. Jesus illustrated this in Matthew 7:24-27 when he taught about the wise and foolish builders. He compared them by saying that when we build on sand (man-made foundations), it falls when winds and rain beat against it. But, when we build on the Rock (Jesus), it stands against anything. Psalm 127: 1 says *"Unless the Lord builds the house, its builder labor in vain"*. Ephesians 2:20 tells us that Jesus is the Cornerstone. When we trust in Jesus, our Rock, we have security even if our world comes crashing down here on earth. We can rely on God's fences of security because our spiritual house is built on the eternal foundation which is Christ.

Psalm 145:13: *"Your kingdom is an everlasting kingdom, and your dominion endures through all generations."*

Daniel 7:14: *"He [Jesus] was given authority, glory and sovereign power; all peoples, nations and men of every language worshiped Him. His dominion is an everlasting dominion that will not pass way, and his kingdom is one that will never be destroyed."*

Isaiah 26:4: *"Trust in the Lord forever, for the Lord, the Lord, is the Rock eternal."*

CHAPTER THREE

MAYHEM AND MIRACLES
(GOD WORKS IN THE FACE OF IMPOSSIBILITIES)

Miracles are events that happen; not by natural means, but by supernatural means which are usually physically and humanly unexplainable. They happen all around us and sometimes we don't even notice. Perhaps it's a simple re-direction of your path to take another route and in doing so, God prevented you from getting into an accident. Sometimes, it's a small quick decision to stay in the lane you were in for a couple of minutes longer instead of changing into the next lane when all of a sudden a car comes out of nowhere behind you, going at a fast rate of speed and flies past you in the lane you were about to change into. Other times it may be a small still voice which tells you to go this way or that. But sometimes the miracle can be more direct, like someone you were praying for survives an illness or is healed from a disease. Some believe the birth of a baby is a miracle which I also tend to believe. As devastating as it was, it would even seem like a miracle happened for anyone to have survived the falling of the twin towers in New York on 911; but many did. I've heard of many stories about those survivors; some inside the buildings; even some who were supposed to be at work that day but for some reason wasn't or perhaps left the building to go get coffee at a diner down the street right before the planes hit. My brother-in-law happened to be in a hotel near the twin towers but left the day before to return home because he had finished his work in one of the towers. Was it a coincidence? Was it luck? Was it happenstance? It is not when God is involved and in control.

      The greatest miracle was the sign of the Messiah coming to Earth through the virgin birth of Mary. Isaiah says in Isaiah 7:14 *"Therefore the Lord himself will give you a sign: the virgin will be with child and will give birth to a son and will call Him Immanuel."* While Jesus was on Earth, He performed many miracles. He turned water into wine, walked on water, calmed the sea, fed multitudes with just a handful of barley loaves and a couple of small fish, healed the sick and even raised the dead to life to name just a few.

      The book of John tells about one such miracle when He healed a man that was born blind. Jesus took some spittle and dirt from the ground, rubbed it on the man's eyes and told him to go wash his eyes at the pool of Siloam. The man did what Jesus told him to do and he could see for the first time in his life. Since the man had been blind since birth, the miracle wasn't just to 'restore' his sight but to 'create' sight. Jesus told His disciples that the man had been blind, not because he had sinned but so that the work of God might be displayed in his life. God's fences of providence, healing grace and triumph was seen in this circumstance. Through Christ's compassion and the man's faith, a life-changing miracle took place. What eternal affect this must have had on this man! How about those who witnessed this miracle? This great act of kindness and grace that Jesus bestowed upon this blind man provided not only healing of sight but a renewing of his soul.

That's what God wants for all of His children. He wants to display His work in all of our lives so that we and others can see God's miraculous power. When we walk in His ways, fully trust Him and put all of our reliance on Him, despite the impossibilities, His work will be displayed in us and through us.

My husband experienced this through a miracle that took place at his birth, as well as other miracles later in his life. My husband's parents describe the night he was born as the 'night of miracles'. He was born two and a half months early, weighing just two pounds four ounces. He had one chance in a million to live. His parents took him home when he was two months old. At that time, he weighed only five pounds which worried them, but the doctor reassured them that he was doing fine. During the week that followed, they didn't think that he was doing as well as he should. At that point, he had dropped back down to two pounds. After talking to the doctor several times, they were reassured again that he was okay and there was no need to bring him into the doctor's office. On the ninth day they called the doctor twice but both times the doctor reassured them that they were worrying needlessly. On the tenth day, they called the doctor again and told him that they thought the baby was dying. After several more calls to the doctor's office, the doctor flat out refused to see him and told them that the baby was too small to live any way; that he had sent him home to die and a trip out would be a waste of time. Now, being a parent myself, I can imagine what his parents were feeling and the anger they must have felt toward this so-called doctor.

They called the closest hospital which was twenty six miles away. My husband's parents were told to quickly get the baby there, that they would have the incubator ready and would notify the highway patrol of the situation. So they all jumped into his uncle's car with his dad holding the baby in the back seat and his mom, aunt and uncle in the front seat. His dad got mad that they were going too slow until he looked at the speedometer and realized that that old car was actually going 95 miles an hour. In fact, they were going so fast and furious that the highway patrol couldn't even catch up with them. By the time they reached the edge of town, my husband's eyes were rolling back into his eye sockets and his lips were starting to turn blue. They were going so fast that when they reached the hospital, the car turned the corner on two wheels. As soon as the car settled down on all four wheels, it passed the hospital by one half block before stopping. But, even before the car was stopped, his dad had already jumped out with son's dying body in his arms and ran up the steps to the hospital three at a time. The nurse met them at the top of the stairs and literally threw the baby into an incubator, turned the oxygen on full blast and he gasped for breath. The hospital doctor stayed with my husband the entire night watching his vitals and praying. This doctor, who stayed with this infant all night, had the tenacity and enormous faith and hope that God would do something miraculous. This must have caused God to smile. God answered his prayer because He had plans for this baby. God's fences of providence and power overshadowed man's frailty, weakness and the impossibility of the grave situation.

My husband did live and grew to be six feet six inches tall. Later in years, I would have loved to been able to take my husband back to that "so-called doctor" who left him for dead, so I could show him that God had the final word – not him. Miracle? I would say so. God did have the last word.

That was just the beginning of miracles during my husband's life. The next miracle happened while trying to protect the neighborhood kids and his own brother, who was six years younger, on the street where he lived. When he was in high school, his younger brother was being picked on by another boy. One day after school, the other boy followed his brother home and picked a fight with him. When my husband came home from school, he found the boy beating on his brother in his front yard so he quickly pulled the boy off of him and flung the boy out into the street. The boy then turned and angrily said "You'll be sorry you did that!" and then he ran off.

My husband didn't think anything more about it and went out in the street to play with all the other neighborhood kids. A short time later, much to everyone's surprise, the boy showed back up on a bicycle. He rode up to my husband and pulled a gun out of his pants pocket. Being concerned about all the other kids that were out playing, he tried to get the boy to put the gun away. All of a sudden, my husband felt a burning sensation in his chest, but still trying to protect the kids around him, took off running toward the boy on the bike. The boy turned white as a ghost and took off peddling as fast as he could with my husband in pursuit. When the biker turned the corner out of the neighborhood, my husband stopped chasing him and turned to go back home. When he did, all the kids started saying "Oh, look!" That's when my husband looked down and his entire shirt was soaked in blood. He then realized that he had been shot in the chest.

He went home and called his mom, who was at work at the time. When she answered she said "What's wrong?" It seemed that she always knew when something bad had happened even before her children said anything. He responded "I'm ok. I've just been shot". It was dead silence on the other end of the phone. Apparently, his mom was in shock and someone had to drive her to the hospital.

My husband drove himself to the emergency room and walked up to the check-in nurse. The lady didn't even look up as she said "What's your problem?" He got her full attention when he told her that he'd been shot. She looked up and saw his blood-soaked shirt and rushed him into a treatment room. They cut off his shirt, examined him, cleaned up his wound, took X-rays which showed where the bullet was and then he waited for the doctor. Several minutes later, the doctor came into the room with the X-rays in his hand, looked at him, looked at the X-rays, got a puzzled look on his face and walked out of the room. A minute later, he came back into the room and asked "Aren't you the guy who was shot?" My husband said he was and the doctor looked dumbfounded. The doctor said "I just don't understand it". The X-ray showed a bullet in his chest but he could no longer see a wound." It was completely gone. So was the bullet. According to the X-ray, the bullet came within inches of his heart. Humanly speaking, a bullet entered his chest, there was blood, a wound and a bullet and there was an X-ray to prove it. Supernaturally speaking, there was definitely divine intervention and it was unexplainable. The doctor wondered what he should put on the report. My husband responded "Just put down 'Miracle' ".

    God's fences of power, providence and protection all came into play in both of these circumstances. God's eternal plan will not be thwarted no matter how impossible the circumstances seem to man. By no will or plan of his own, God showed mercy to my husband through these two miraculous events. God's plan was to make sure my husband survived in order to make a difference and impact in his life to all who he encountered throughout his journey. God blessed many lives through these miracles. I'm sure the hospital doctor's faith increased when he saw the baby live despite the grave circumstances. I'm sure the ER doctor who saw the miracle of the gunshot wound saw God at work, causing him to look at future situations like that in a different way. It may have even caused him to turn to God himself and as a result, bring his whole family to the knowledge of the Savior. We may never know how one moment in time will change one life or many lives. That's when God's fences of providence comes into play. Through all of our human efforts, they always fall short of God's glory.

God saved my husband's life to fulfill His plan for him to eventually call him to the ministry. He pastored a church in Kansas for a year and a half. Later in ministry, my husband was hired to teach a high school class at a Korean Church in California because the kids mainly spoke English. Sunday after Sunday my husband would come home afterwards feeling defeated because he didn't think he was getting through to them or making a difference in their lives. He felt that all of his efforts were fruitless. A couple of months after he passed away, I received a phone call from one of those students. They told me that because of my husband and what he taught them, he and several other of my husband's students decided to attend Christian Bible School. God is amazing! I was blessed and praised God to know that because my husband lived, many other lives were touched at that church. My husband would have been blessed knowing that his teaching did have a life-changing impact on his students despite his doubt and discouragement. Although my husband didn't see it at the time, God's fences of miraculous providence was still working in the hearts of those teenagers.

Despite all of my husband's faults and failures, God still had His hand on his life. I myself, was not aware of these kind of dramatic life and death supernatural events in my life, but I still trust in God and His plan for my life. Jeremiah 29:11 says *"For I know the plans I have for you, declares the Lord, plans to prosper you and not to harm you, plans to give you hope and a future."* God has reassured me through His Word that He loves me for who I am but yet sees me as what I can become, which leads me to the conclusion that I still have a lot of learning to do until He takes me home. Despite all of my faults and failures, God still brings many miracles into my life as well as yours, even when we can't see them. God's fences of protection and miraculous power still surrounds us in every situation. We just have to look for them.

     Miracles happen so that everyone might know the power of the Lord. Pharaoh learned about God's power when God's people were in enslaved in Egypt for four hundred years. God heard their cries for deliverance and He assigned Moses the task to go to Pharaoh, with the help of his brother Aaron, to free God's people. When Moses showed up at the scene by God's direction, Pharaoh, believing he was stronger than any powerful deity, was used to having the enslaved Israelites doing all the work and he didn't want that to end any time soon. But God had other plans. Despite nine plagues brought upon the Egyptians, which was directed at all of Egypt's gods, Pharaoh's stubbornness continued until after the tenth plague when the Lord struck down all the firstborn in Egypt no matter the status, even the Pharaoh's son. Exodus 12:31 tells of Pharaoh's submission to let God's people leave Egypt. In fact, the Egyptians told them to hurry and leave or they may die. They were afraid of God's power if they didn't allow them to leave. So God led Moses and the Israelites out to the desert to camp by the Red Sea. Now you may wonder, like a lot of Israelites did, as to why God would lead them to a "dead end" where they would be hemmed in. Well, God had plans for that too. Although

God brought them out of Egypt with His mighty hand, He wasn't done showing His power.

Exodus 14:3-4 *"Pharaoh will think, 'The Israelites were wandering around the land in confusion, hemmed in by the desert '. And I [God] will harden Pharaoh's heart, and he will pursue them. But I will gain glory for myself through Pharaoh and all his army, and the Egyptians will know that I am the Lord."*

So Pharaoh and his army pursued them and when they found them at the edge of the waters of the Red Sea, they thought sure they could overtake them. But again, they underestimated God of the Israelites. The scripture tells us in Exodus 14:19-20 *"Then the angel of God, who had been traveling in front of Israel's army, withdrew and went behind them. The pillar of cloud also moved from in front and stood behind them, coming between the armies of Egypt and Israel. Throughout the night the cloud brought darkness to the one side and light to the other side; so neither went near the other all night long."* After Moses reassured the people, he followed God's direction and raised his staff and hand over the sea and all that night the Lord drove the sea back with a strong east wind and turned it into dry land.

Exodus 14:16 *"Raise your staff and stretch out your hand over the sea to divide the water so that the Israelites can go through the sea on dry ground. I will harden the hearts of the Egyptians so that they will go in after them. And I will gain glory through Pharaoh and all his army, through his chariots and his horsemen. The Egyptians will know that I am the Lord when I gain glory through Pharaoh, his chariots and his horsemen."*

God showed His ultimate boundless no nonsense incomprehensible power to Egypt and to Israel in these verses. These miracles not only revealed God's divine control over nature, but He also showed His fences of Providence and Protection.

Just as a reminder, here are many Biblical accounts of the Omnipotent God at work:

- He split the Red Sea so the Israelites can walk through on dry land: Exodus 14:13-31
- He brought down the walls of Jericho: Joshua 5:13-6:20
- He turned water into wine: John 2:1-11
- He walked on water: Matthew 14:25
- He calmed the sea: Mark 4:35-39; Matthew 8:23-27
- He healed many: Matthew 15:30-31
- He had power over demons: Matthew 8:28-34; Mark 1:23-25, 9:14-27
- He has power over principalities and powers: Ephesians1:18-23; Colossians 1:15-20, 2:10

Matthew 19:26b says *"With God all things are possible"*. No one but God could split a sea, bring down walls, turn water into wine, walk on water, have power over waves, bring healing to many, remove demons, bring life to a dying baby or make a bullet disappear. When God's power gets involved, unexplainable miracles happen. Sometimes we see them clearly; sometimes they are subtle.

But even when we don't see them at all, God is still working. If you don't believe me, then believe Jesus when He said in John 5:17 *"My Father is always at his Work to this very day, and I, too, am working."* We just have to be open and expectant for those unexpected miracles.

Blind Faith

(Taken from John 9)

A darkened world was all I've known
Perhaps its fate or sin I've sown
I beg for mercy in my strife
From those who daily passes by.
Each wakened hour my fears succeed
I have no wants, but only needs.
I have no hope but still I wait
For someone's help, outside the gate.

The Pharisees who came my way
Judged my state, then walked away;
But when a man from Galilee
Walked by, he stopped in front of me.
"Light of the World" I heard with fear,
Of what he'd do when he drew near.
He seemed to understand my plight
He said he'd give me back my sight.

Unsure of what he'd said was true,
I did just as he told me to.
I washed the mud off from my eyes;
My sight returned, to my surprise;
But those around could not perceive
What the man had done for me.
For I was blind and now I see
But those with sight, could not believe.

For they were listening to their pride
Instead of letting God inside.
Although their sight had always been
They were really blind with fear and sin.
But God looks right into the heart
From where all of our actions start.
With open eyes, God made me see
But with my heart I now believe.

@Catherine Garrett
July 30, 1996

CHAPTER FOUR

FEELINGS AND FAITH

(SEEING IN THE DARK WITHOUT A FLASHLIGHT)

As I've mentioned before, I felt a lot of insecurities in my early life; in school and even during my early days of marriage. During the time when my husband was a pastor in a local church in Kansas, our church hosted the summer Vacation Bible School (VBS). Because I was the pastor's wife, I was expected to be in charge of that event. Up to that point, I have never been in charge of any event or even felt like I was a leader in anything. Naturally, I felt more secure as a follower than a leader so I was very nervous about this responsibility. I didn't feel confident to do what was necessary in order for the VBS to be successful. I was in charge of choosing the curriculum, organizing the crafts and supplies and selecting the teachers. I was certainly feeling the burden and insecurity about the whole thing until I realized that it wasn't actually "I" who was doing the work but it was God who was doing the work. It was HIS Vacation Bible School; not mine. I recognized that I was looking only to my feelings and lack of confidence instead of faith in God and His great resources, in order to succeed. I was trying to do everything on my own instead of depending on Him, His resources and fences of provision. My weakness became His strength.

Once I put aside my doubt and uncertainty, I put my trust and faith in God to take over, I was amazed on how smoothly the planning, organizing and completion of the event went. Not only was the VBS successful, but I also learned the important lesson of faith versus feelings. God constantly brings Bible verses to my remembrance when He is teaching me this life-long lesson. One verse that is the top of the list is Hebrews 11:1 *"Now faith is being sure of what we hope for and certain of what we do not see."* Second on the list is Proverbs 3:5 and 6 *"Trust in the Lord with all your heart and lean not on your own understanding; in all your ways acknowledge him, and he will make your paths straight."* Once I acknowledged Him in the process, He certainly made my path straight and as a result, the event was successful and my trust in God grew. All in all, I'd say it was a win-win for everyone. He showed me that if I put my trust in His fences of strength and provision instead of my human strength and resources, God can do amazing things. Jeremy 32:17 says *"Ah, Sovereign Lord, you have made the heavens and the earth by your great power and outstretched arm. Nothing is too hard for you."*

A man named Abram certainly demonstrated Hebrews 11:1. In Genesis, God called Abram to leave his country, his people and his father's household and go to the land God will show him. God promised him that He would make Abram a great nation and bless him and all the peoples on earth through him. That calling would be a bit scary for me and I would have felt very insecure if I were in his shoes, or should I say sandals. But Abram's actions reflected his total faith in God's fences of protection and providence, and what God directed him to do, even though he had no idea where God wanted him to go. He put aside his feelings for faith in a God he didn't even see and go to a land where he hadn't been before. He totally yielded to God's will and guidance even in the midst of the unknown.

    The Bible says that Abram left as directed by God. It appeared that there was no apprehension on the part of Abram to go when God said 'go' despite the unknown path ahead of him. No insecurity. No doubt. Just faith; faith in God's direction and God's promises and God rewarded him for it. In Genesis 15:6 it says *"Abram believed the Lord and he credited it to him as righteousness"*. God eventually led him to the Promised Land and God blessed him just as He had promised.

    Some may say that Abram just had blind faith but that's not the case. His faith was based upon God's Word and promises to make him into a great nation, make his name great and all the peoples of the earth would be blessed through him. He stepped out with that assurance knowing that God would direct him as to where he should go, just as God had promised. He didn't get wrapped up with the unknown journey that God laid before him. He just trusted in God's fences of protection, providence, guidance and mercy. God's fences were seen throughout his journey and He fulfilled His promises, as He does for all His children. Because of God's promise to make him a great nation, his name was changed to Abraham, which meant "Father of many".

When I was young and living on the farm, I was really scared of the dark. The country at night can get so dark that you literally can't see the hand right in front of your face. The outhouse, which was surrounded by bushes, sat on the east side of the long circular driveway. At night, the only light we had on our way to the outhouse at night was a yard light which was by the driveway in front of the house. As we drew closer to the outhouse and out of the range of the yard light, we had to use a flashlight to guide our steps through the dark bushy areas until we safely reached our destination. Even though I had familiarity with that area, I still could have lost my footing if I had not have had the light of the flashlight onto my path. Just as the flashlight was a guide on my physical path, God's word is the flashlight on our spiritual path. In Psalm 119:105 *"God's word is a lamp to my feet and a light for my path."*

When we continue studying and trusting God's Word, He will guide us on the path we should go. Just like Abraham, He'll give us wisdom and direction if we just trust Him. We can't see ahead of us but God is Omnipresent. He is behind us, beside us and goes before us. Psalm 139:8-12 *"If I go up to the heavens, you are there; if I make my bed in the depths, you are there. If I rise on the wings of the dawn, if I settle on the far side of the sea, even there your hand will guide me, your right hand will hold me fast. If I say, surely the darkness will hide me and the light become night around me, even the dark will not be dark to you; the night will shine like the day, for darkness is as light to you."*

Despite of all of God's promises, I still doubt and worry at times. When I am faced with situations, I still sometimes go by feelings instead of faith in God's fences of promises of His presence; even in the future I haven't even seen yet. How will I get out of debt? Where will I obtain the finances to publish this book? Where will I live after I retire? Will I have enough money to retire? As I have said before, I'm still learning the lesson of faith and I can bet when the next circumstance arises, my faith will have to be tested again. But thankfully God is patient in the lesson.

As all humans do, Jonah was slow to learn a very big lesson and as a result, he found himself in a lot of hot water or should I say deep water. In fact, this was such a great lesson to us all, that Jonah's lesson was recorded in the entire book of Jonah.

Jonah was God's prophet. In the first chapter of Jonah, the Lord came to Jonah and said *"Go to the great city of Nineveh and preach against it, because its wickedness has come up before me."* But Jonah ran away from the Lord because he knew the people of Nineveh were very wicked and he didn't want to go. Instead of having faith in God's direction in his life, he went by his own feelings. He knew that if he preached to them according to God's Word, that they might be remorseful and ask for God's forgiveness. And, when they did, God would forgive them. He didn't feel that they deserved God's mercy and forgiveness. I'll have to admit that sometimes I feel that way about sinful evil people too and hope that God would punish them rather than forgive them. Then I remember I'm also a sinner and I too needed His forgiveness. Sin can't compete with God's Grace. Romans 5:20b *"But where sin increased, Grace increased all the more."*

The Bible tells us that Jonah jumped onto a boat heading for Tarsus, which is in the opposite direction of Nineveh. During this boat trip, the Lord sent a great wind on the sea. It was such a violent storm that the ship threatened to break apart. All the sailors were afraid and each prayed to their own god. They started throwing the cargo into the sea to lighten the ship. But Jonah went down below deck and fell into a deep sleep. The captain went down and woke him up and told him to get up and call upon his God so they won't perish.

The sailors cast lots to find out who on board was responsible for the calamity. When the lot fell on Jonah, he admitted that he was the one responsible because he worships the Lord, the maker of Heaven, who made the sea and the land. Jonah told them that he was running away from the Lord. Meanwhile the sea grew rougher and rougher so they asked Jonah what they should do to make the sea calm down. Jonah told them that because it was his fault, they should pick him up and throw him into the sea. Then, it will become calm again.

Despite all the sailors' efforts by throwing more and more cargo off the ship and trying to row the ship back to shore, the sea grew wilder and wilder. No matter how hard they tried, they couldn't appease the storm's anger. So, they did what Jonah asked. When they threw him overboard into the stormy sea, it immediately became calm.

When Jonah entered into the depths of the water, God provided a great fish to swallow him. While he was inside the fish for three days and three nights, he called out to the Lord. When he admitted sinning against the Lord and asked for forgiveness, the Lord answered. God heard his cry and redeemed him from the heart of the sea. The Lord immediately commanded the fish to vomit up Jonah onto dry land. This reveals God's control over nature and also that He forgives us when we ask for forgiveness. God is omnipotent and merciful.

This experience certainly changed Jonah's mind and attitude. It certainly would mine. He immediately obeyed the Lord's command and headed for Nineveh to proclaim God's message. Jonah finally obeyed the Word of the Lord and told them that God would destroy them in forty days if they didn't turn from their wickedness. The Ninevites, from the greatest to the least, believed God and fasted and prayed. They called on the name of the Lord to have compassion on them, to turn away His fierce anger and relent from their destruction. When God saw their repentant hearts and how they turned from their evil ways, He had compassion on them and did not bring the destruction on them as He had threatened.

Despite Jonah's human feelings, he experienced God's fences of protection, compassion and obedience. Even though it appeared that the Ninevites were hopelessly lost in their sins, they experienced God's fences of mercy and forgiveness.

Psalm 103:8, 10-13: *"The Lord is compassionate and gracious, slow to anger, abounding in love. He does not treat us as our sins deserve or repay us according to our iniquities. For as high as the heavens are above the earth, so great is His love for those who fear Him; as far as the east is from the west, so far has He removed our transgressions from us. As a father has compassion on His children, so the Lord has compassion on those who fear Him."* Jonah or the people of Nineveh didn't deserve God's compassion or forgiveness. We don't either. When we mess up, sometimes over and over because we don't learn the lesson the first time, God never gives up on us. He is always compassionate, patient and forgives us because of His great love.

Ephesians 2:4 *"But because of His great love for us, God, who is rich in mercy, made us alive with Christ even when we were dead in transgressions – it is by grace you have been saved."*

I love heights. Once in a while I would climb up one of the silos behind the barn, go to the very top and sit for hours; pretending I was a giant. When I'm on the ground standing by the silo, I was only able to see the fences at the outskirts of the farm. But when I climbed up on the top of the silo, I can see for miles and miles beyond the fences. Looking back at that now reminds me that I can only see what is here and now but God can see everything beyond what I see; even what lies ahead. Most of the time, because I can't see what God is doing, I get lost in my feelings or circumstances instead of trusting God. But I believe that when God brings me to those unexpected places of life, He's preparing me for the next lesson of faith. God is ever near; behind me, beside me, before me. Jesus' parting words to his disciples and to us today in Matthew 28:20b is *"And surely I will be with you always, even to the end of the age."*

CHAPTER FIVE
FOLIES AND FOOTSTEPS
(MULES DON'T TALK)

When I was a senior in high school, I met a guy that I really liked. He was very polite and nice. Considering I was still feeling insecure about myself, I was blown away at how this guy accepted me as I was and made me feel special. He was a cute, blond haired guy and I thought I was 'in love'. Of course, love to a high school student isn't 'real love'. Butterflies don't always mean true love just like rainclouds in the distance doesn't mean there will be rain over my house. There was one problem with that relationship I was about to embark on. He was of a denomination that my parents didn't agree with; and if I was honest with myself, I wouldn't have agreed with either if I would have thought with my brain instead of my heart. But nonetheless, I attended his school dance and then he was my date for my senior prom. All the popular girls at my dance was swooning over him and were asking me who he was and where I met him, which I thought was pretty funny considering that I wasn't among the popular crowd. Selfishly, I was glad I had something they didn't have for a change, and at that point, I felt accepted and special; like I was popular too.

We saw each other a few times after that and wrote each other quite often throughout the summer months. I was hopeful that our relationship would grow but time would tell otherwise. After a while, when I would try to go see him, he wouldn't be home at that particular time. The same thing happened when he came by to see me. Pretty soon we just couldn't get together for one reason or another and his letters to me started to decrease in time. I just couldn't understand it. Why wasn't God allowing me to see him? It was just as if God didn't want us to continue this relationship. God said "no" and I felt that it wasn't fair and I was angry at God about it. He was the most respectful guy I've ever known so why couldn't we be together? At the time, it just didn't make sense to me.

      Although I was unhappy about those uncontrollable circumstances, time passed and I went on with life. In hindsight (which is usually the case), I eventually realized that God did have a reason for keeping us apart, even if I didn't see it at the time. I know now that if I would have continued pursuing that relationship, I would have had to join his denomination even though my beliefs were much different than his. God reminded me in Proverbs 20:24 that a man's (or woman's) steps are directed by the Lord. Yes, we make our choices but sometimes if those choices are not good for us, His fences of providence and protection takes precedence for our own good, whether we know it at the time or not. Proverbs 19:21 also says *"Many are the plans in a man's heart, but it is the Lord's purpose that prevails."*

When God said "no" to that relationship, He had a better plan for me that I couldn't see at the time. He had a better perspective and knew that the path I was walking on would not be good for me. He knew what the future consequences would be if my plans had been fulfilled to continue that relationship. That's why God's answer to prayer is sometimes "no". Hindsight has always been a great teacher for me. It's too bad that I couldn't have learned this lesson at the time. Even though I hadn't yet surrendered my life to Jesus as my Lord and Savior, He knew I still needed to learn that I could trust God because he is good and is always motivated by love. Psalm 25:8 *"Good and upright is the Lord; therefore He instructs sinners in His ways."* Even before I knew Him, He knew me and was preparing me for my future journey to walk with Him. In every circumstance, God was teaching me through each lesson of faith. He was teaching me not to trust in my own human feelings and plans but to trust in His divine leading and purpose for my life. He was also protecting me from distress and hardship. He guarded my past and present footsteps as well as my future ones. He kept me on the straight and narrow road with His Words of truth. Psalm 121:3 says *"He will not let your foot slip - He who watches over you will not slumber."*

My circumstance with making the wrong decision with the wrong guy, reminded me about another guy named Balaam, who was also facing a bad decision and how God intervened in quite an amazing way. Balaam was a heathen diviner, but also possessed some knowledge of the true God. Although he felt that his gifts were derived from God, he became self-conceited and covetous. He would do or say anything for anyone for the right price.

Balak, King of Moab gathered with the Midianites against the Israelites, who were encamped in the plain of Moab. He sent messengers and rewards to Balaam asking him to go and curse the Israelites for him, hoping that it would bring victory to Balak's army over them. After Balaam declined, Balak's messengers returned with more rewards and honor, promising anything he wanted if he would go and curse them. With the great temptation before him, Balaam agreed to talk to the Israelites but he told them that he could do nothing contrary to the command of the Lord his God. During the night, God told him to go ahead and go, but say only what God wants him to say. Although God gave Balaam permission to go and Balaam knew he was supposed to say only the words of God, God was angry with Balaam because He knew Balaam's heart. God knew that Balaam's lust was the real reason and motive to go as Balak requested. Perhaps with the lure of rewards and honor, he would decide to curse Israel as Balak wanted him to do instead of blessing them as God directed. This is where it gets really interesting.

    According to Numbers 22, the next morning Balaam saddled up his donkey and started off with Balak's messengers. But because of God's anger towards Balaam, the angel of the Lord stood in the road to kill him. As Balaam and two servants were riding along, Balaam's donkey suddenly saw the angel of the Lord standing in the road with a drawn sword blocking his way. She bolted off the road into a field, but Balaam beat her back onto the road. The road they were on had two vineyard walls on each side. The donkey squirmed past the angel by pressing against the wall, crushing Balaam's foot in the process. So he beat her again. Then the angel of the Lord moved farther down the road and stood in a place so narrow that the donkey couldn't get by at all. So she lay down in the road.

In a great fit of anger Balaam beat her again with his staff. Then the Lord caused the donkey to speak! "What have I done that deserves your beating me these three times?"

Now, if your donkey or household pet or any other animal started talking to you, you may have many reactions such as unbelief, thought you were dreaming, shocked, confused or just wanted to run away. Not Balaam. Crazy as it sounds, he started a conversation with his donkey! He answered by shouting at her, "Because you have made me look like a fool! I wish I had a sword with me, for I would kill you." Then the donkey responds with a question. "Have I ever done anything like this before in my entire life?" "No" Balaam admitted. Then the Lord opened Balaam's eyes and he saw the angel standing in the road way with a drawn sword. At that moment, Balaam fell flat on the ground before him.

The angel asked why he was beating his donkey three times and told him that he was there to stop him because he was heading for destruction. The angel continued by saying that three times the donkey saw him and shed away from him or otherwise he would have killed Balaam and spared his donkey. Then Balaam confessed that he had sinned and told the angel that he would go back home if he doesn't want him to go. But the angel instructed him to go and tell the people only what God tells him to say. Much to the chagrin of Balak, Balaam did bless Israel instead of cursing them. Because of this, Balak was livid with rage towards Balaam.

Despite Balak's efforts and even Balaam's intent to disobey God, God's plan was not thwarted. Despite human effort, God's plan cannot be changed. He is the same yesterday, today and forever. God is not a man; that He should lie. (Numbers 21:19) Balaam's footsteps became a folly to him. Although he thought he was on the right path, God knew that it was the wrong path that would lead to destruction. It was the same with me and that boy that I thought I was in love with. God placed an obstacle and roadblock in my path because it wasn't the one that God wanted me to marry and it certainly would have led to the destruction of my Christian beliefs. I am thankful today that God stopped me but I'm also thankful that God didn't have to use an angel with a sword to do it! God provided me with fences of protection, providence and mercy.

God does work in mysterious ways! They are certainly beyond human understanding. God had to teach me another lesson of faith, which was similar to Balaam's story, when He gave me a directive that I didn't want to follow. In fact, I was downright stubborn about it. It had only been a few months after I graduated from high school and surrendered my life to the Lord. God was still teaching me His Word to live by so I was still what some call being a "Baby" in Christ. I was still on the milk, slowly learning daily the truth in His Word and Biblical life applications. I wasn't into the meat of the Word yet; nor really understood what it meant to be totally surrendered to Jesus, His Word and His will. It happened when I started working as a baby-sitter with a local family after high school.

I had been working as the family's baby-sitter for a few months when I found out that their relative, who lived in Oklahoma City needed a live-in baby-sitter, which today would be called a Nanny. I thought it would be a great opportunity to get out of the small town I was in and go to a bigger city so I took the job. It was late summer, early fall, and had been working for just about two to three months. I found that I really liked the area and found a good church to worship. Then out of the blue, the husband of the family found out that he was being transferred to California. California! Wow! I've always wanted to go there! They invited me to continue in the job and wanted me to go to California with them; even paying for my hotel and food along with way. We arrived in sunny California and I was totally excited.

Well, I just settled into the 'good life' in sunny California and was having a great time. It was great weather and I loved the area we lived in. We could see the mountains from our back yard. I got involved with a local church and made some Christian friends. It was wonderful; a dream come true for me. It was certainly better than my in-the-middle-of-nowhere small town in Kansas (remember, I was just a teenager). I could hardly believe how nice and comfortable it was. I was there for only a few months when the unthinkable happened.

God told me to go home. No!!!!! What does God mean, go home? It couldn't be. I must have heard it wrong. I must have been getting the wrong message. I just got there! I liked it there! Of course, I immediately said 'No' to God. Can you imagine that? If you've ever said 'No' to

God, you soon discover that He will not take no for answer. (Remember Jonah?) Both Jonah and I eventually found out that there was so much more at stake than what we refuse to see. God always has a better plan around the corner. For a whole week, I dug in my heels of stubbornness, refused to yield to His command and said 'No' but God persisted. I was disobedient, miserable and worn out from fighting with God (remember when Jacob wrestled with God and Jacob got a painful hip out of it?) At the end of a week of wrestling, I couldn't take it anymore and finally just gave in. Immediately I was amazed to find that my burden that I carried all week was lifted off my shoulders. When I said 'Yes' to God, freedom was restored and I felt peace again. Unknown to me, when God said "no" to my staying where I was in California, He had a better plan and purpose because He had a better perspective. Again, God placed His fences of protection and providence around me, even if I didn't see them. I didn't know at the time why God would want me to go back to a small home town with no opportunities, but I obeyed. But what I couldn't see at the time, God had many future opportunities in store for me as I would soon find out.

    I was home for about a week when a new minister in town came for a visit. During his visit he asked me if I wanted to go to college. I actually chuckled to myself because at that point in my life, I had endured twelve long years of school and wanted nothing more to do with further education. When I replied that I wasn't planning on going to college, he handed me a brochure for a school in Oklahoma City, 'just in case I'd change my mind about going to go to college'. I graciously took it but immediately set it aside and didn't think any more about it. Makes you wonder why I didn't just throw it away all together, huh? Again, God's providence. About a week later, I came across the brochure underneath everything on my dresser. I started thinking that by attending this school it would be my opportunity to get out of this town; not because that a college education was a positive thing and would help me toward a career. Although I was doubtful that I could get any financial assistance, I applied anyway. Much to my surprise, I was able to get a loan and a grant. This was certainly a confirmation that God wanted me to go and I was happy to go.

I didn't see it at the time but God had a plan. He wanted me to come home so I can be at home to get that college brochure from the new minister in town, then find that brochure a week later and place the desire in my heart to attend that college. Timing and location were God's tools because at that college, I met my husband. I've discovered that when God has a plan, He works on both ends. God worked on both ends for me and my husband to make sure both of us were there at the God-ordained time. Psalm 18:30 *"As for God, His way is perfect, the word of the Lord is flawless."* Deuteronomy 32:4 *"He is the Rock, His works are perfect, and all His ways are just."*

I was arriving on campus for the second semester with just a suitcase, a guitar and a lot of insecurities. I didn't know anyone there and it was a little scary. I settled into my dorm room and went out to the lobby where lots of kids were sitting and chatting. I was too scared to talk to anyone so I just sat down in one of the big stuffed chairs to survey all the activity in the room. Out of nowhere, a guy sat down next to me on the other stuffed chair and started talking to me. "You're from Kansas aren't you?" Boy was my mind spinning and my nervousness raised from a six to a ten on the insecurity scale. I was hesitant to respond but I finally asked, "How can you tell? Is it the way I dressed?" Since I was from a small hick town in Kansas, I figured that my attire didn't conform to the modern attire of a bigger city. He then responded, "No, a little birdie told me." At that point, my insecurity got the best of me and I quickly got up and went back to my room. I found out later that the home town pastor's brother, who also attended this college told many on campus that a girl was coming from Kansas the second semester. One of those people he told was the guy in the stuffed chair in the lobby that I was talking to. Much to my surprise, I found out after a couple of years of marriage that it was actually my husband was that guy in that stuffed chair when I told him about that incident.

  My husband-to-be had already been there for the first semester, during which time, he acquired food poisoning. He developed an extremely high temperature which was so high the doctors recommended that he should go home to recover for a year before going back to school. But he was a stubborn man and decided not to follow their recommendations. He went back to school the second semester because his parents had already paid for it. We met second semester when he returned and I arrived. God's plan was not to be thwarted no matter the circumstances in both of our lives. He removed all roadblocks to complete that plan. Sometimes God builds roadblocks and sometimes he removes them. God uses closed doors as well as open doors.

When I was saying 'No' to God back in Oklahoma, little did I realize that just in a few months after finally saying 'Yes', I would be in the right place at the right time. My footsteps led only by God can result in perfect harmony with God's will. It was at that college that my husband where God confirmed to both of us that we were going to get married. When our footsteps are aligned with God's, our paths are straight and unhindered. Proverbs 4:11 and 12 says *"I guide you in the way of wisdom and lead you along straight paths. When you walk, your steps will not be hampered; when you run, you will not stumble."* Also, in Proverbs 16:9 *"In his heart, man plans his course, but the Lord determines his steps."*

I'm sure you've discovered too that life doesn't always turn out as we plan. There may be disappointments, detours and U-turns but God is never early and never late. Whether we see it, understand it or agree with it, He is always right on time. He doesn't work on our time frame but within the scope of His providence. God uses all things, even negative circumstances, to accomplish His glorious life-changing plans; even when we say 'No' to Him. Whether we want to admit it at the time, all of His plans are good (Jeremiah 29:11), loving (Psalm 25:10) and perfect (II Samuel 22:31). He knows what He's doing! We're much better off when we allow God to do His choosing. He strengthens and deepens our faith one step at a time as we trust His Word and His leading. We can have confidence in His fences of perfect power and perfect timing.

Years ago, I had a hard time deciphering road maps. Today, my map-reading skills are better although I still have trouble with directions. There are many circumstances in all of our lives in which our decisions will have a great impact, good or bad, on the road ahead. Just like road maps and road signs that guide us in the car, God's word can also become our "road sign" and "road map" so to speak, on the road of life. It gives us light ahead as we take each step. It gives us direction and guidance. It gives us warnings. As we read and digest it, it gives us spiritual nourishment. And as we live it, it becomes a light to others. Knowing God's will can sometimes be difficult but when we read and humbly live out His Word and be obedient, He will become our life-line and guide in this very dark scary world. His Word is true and will never end. Jeremiah 29:11 and Romans 8:28 both say God has a good plan for us; even if we don't think it is at the time because we can't see it. God's fences of providence, guidance and perfect timing is always greater than our choices and keeps us in His will.

CHAPTER SIX

REQUIREMENTS AND RESOURCES, TRIALS AND TRIUMPHS

(IT'S ALL ABOUT GOD)

I'll have to admit, having enough resources in our current economy, has been quite stressful. Again, I am learning another lesson of faith by trusting God with every aspect of my life, including finances. I'm sure many other folks are in similar situations and dealing with financial deficiencies of some sort or another. But yet, I still haven't learned to trust God in all circumstances, especially financial ones. I'm so glad God is patient.

It seems like when new uncertain circumstances like these arise, God always brings to my memory a time when He did come through in a difficult time and how He worked; even though I felt helpless. In those circumstances, the same message comes to the forefront. <u>God</u> is my resource!

One such time that He reminds me of how He provided, despite the dire circumstances, was when we lived in Kansas. My husband and my three year old son moved from South Carolina and stayed a couple of years in my home town in Kansas. While we were there, my husband was on disability due to knee surgery and I was seven and a half months pregnant with my second child. Since he was on disability and I wasn't working due to my pregnancy, we had very little money coming in. We were always too proud to ask for assistance from my family or his so we struggled throughout that year; bringing in only two thousand dollars for the entire year. Of course, that was back in the 1970's and living expenses were considerably less than they are now, but even then we struggled. Many days during that year, I felt like I was releasing my last breath and sinking from an impossible situation. The daily struggling to have enough resources felt excruciating…..at least until God stepped in.

    As children always seem to do, my son was very quickly growing out of all of his clothes. As I've told many, both sides of our family have 'tall genes'. My husband stood at six feet six inches and I am six feet tall so we could pretty much guarantee that our children were also going to be tall. I decided to go through all of his dresser drawers and pull out anything that didn't fit him anymore. After I had finished, all I saw were empty dresser drawers just like how my heart and faith felt. There were only a couple of items remaining that would fit him. He had grown out of all of the others. We had no idea what we were going to do. We certainly didn't have any money to buy any more clothes for him. As I stared into all the empty drawers, with all that my faith could muster, I said a quick prayer, "Lord, please provide him some more clothes. Please, we need help!" That was it. But apparently God thought it was enough. We were exhausted, our resources were exhausted and our faith was barely hanging on. At that moment, out of desperation, I went to God, who has unmeasurable resources.

The next Saturday morning, I went out my front door onto my porch to go somewhere. I looked down and there by the door was a brown paper sack. I had no idea where this sack came from or who put it there, but when I opened it up, much to my surprise, there were some children's clothes. And, much to my greater surprise, every one of them fit my son! Wow! I was blown away. God really saw my circumstances and very small mustard-seed faith and answered my humble simple prayer. God is so good! To this day, I still don't know who the person was who placed that sack on my porch but what I do know, it was God-sent in an answer to my prayer.

But, that was the first of many times that we saw God's hand of provision that same year. God reminds me of when Kansas was in a major drought. It hadn't rained for months and there was no rain in sight for my hometown. But in this instance, God took care of us despite the fact we were in a rain drought, as well as a financial drought.

We had a large backyard; just perfect for a vegetable garden, which would supplement our minimal income. We prayed by faith by plotting out our garden on paper; despite the fact that we couldn't even afford the seeds to plant in the garden. On it, we wrote down the exact kind of vegetables we wanted to plant; even being specific as "Blue Lake" green beans. We borrowed my dad's seed catalog and picked out everything we wanted to plant in our garden and placed them on our paper garden. We prayed over our paper garden and waited; trusting in God to provide. By that time, we figured that if God could fill dresser drawers with clothes, he could fill a garden with vegetables.

    On the following weekend, our neighbor knocked on our door. In his hand he held a brown paper bag. He told us that he had noticed that we had a great area in the backyard that would make a great garden spot. Then he handed us the bag, which he said contained extra packets of seeds that he wasn't going to use. He thought that we could use them to plant a garden. We looked inside and found the exact kinds of seeds we had previously picked out in my dad's seed catalog; including "Blue Lake" green beans. God moved in the heart of this neighbor for our provision.

    Despite the ongoing drought, we planted our garden and the plants started popping up above the ground. We were so excited! After months of no rain, the town's water supply was becoming dangerously low. It seemed that every storm cloud that arose on the horizon that appeared to be moving straight for us swerved at the last moment and went right around us as if an invisible hand was at work. Each time that occurred, our hopes dwindled. We finally realized that we started looking at the clouds to provide instead of God, so we turned back and focused on God once again and prayed for rain. But still the clouds kept veering away from us. At this point, we couldn't water our lawns, wash our cars or water our garden. But miraculously, the green beans continued to produce. And boy, did they produce!

    Just about the time that the beans were producing bushels of produce, hundreds of grasshoppers showed up and started attacking our already starving, thirsty plants. They ate every single leaf off of every single beanstalk. We couldn't stop them! But yet again, miraculously, despite the grasshopper's destruction and the continual drought, beans kept growing. And growing. And growing. We picked beans until we had nowhere else to put them. We canned 48 quarts and gave bushels and bushels away. We couldn't pick them fast enough! God kept providing. Besides the eternally producing bean plants, our sweet corn stalks grew to be over seven feet tall and we harvested many ears of corn. All this without water and the overwhelming flood of ravenous grasshoppers!

    Weeks passed and still no rain. At least the grasshoppers finally went away; probably because they ran out of things to eat! Then out of the blue, my uncle, who was our town's mayor, showed up at our front door. He told us that a new well was being dug outside of town and the water was just running onto the ground so it could be tested. He said that if we could find a container, we could go get some water for our garden. But we didn't have any sort of large container or a way to haul the water. We sat down on our front porch and prayed. As we sat there praying and thinking about how we could get the water to our garden, a pickup truck just happened to drive by and stopped in front of our neighbor's house. In the back were some empty 50-gallon drums. Coincidence? I don't think so. We looked at each other, smiled and thanked God. I quickly went over to the man and asked what he was going to do with those drums. He said he was going to throw them away but if I wanted one, I could have one. We placed it in the trunk of our old yellow GMC sedan and headed out to where the well was being dug. We spent all day Saturday and made at least a half a dozen trips from the well to our garden. We hauled the drum of water from the well into town, and then hand carried the water from the drum to the garden using buckets and cooking pots. As you may imagine, we were quite exhausted; considering my husband was still in a cast from a knee surgery and I was seven and one half months' pregnant. We were quite a sight. But what we can say is that God provided and the garden finally got the water it needed.

The next day was Sunday and we were sitting in church next to my aunt. While we were waiting for services to begin, I briefly told her of how we spent our entire Saturday and our tireless efforts to water our garden in the midst of the drought. About midpoint through the service, we noticed some clouds rolling in. Then before we knew it, a clap of thunder sounded; then another. Then a total drenching down pour of rain started. My husband and I looked at each other and just chuckled, along with sighs of relief that rain finally came our way. My aunt then turned to me and said, "I guess God felt sorry for you and for all the work you did yesterday so He decided to help you out."

That might have been true, but what we really saw was God's blessings pouring down in a long awaited summer rain. As a result, our garden got watered; our faith grew as tall as the corn stalks and as abundantly as the "Blue Lake" green beans. The Bible verse we held onto during this time was, Proverbs 3:5 *"Trust in the Lord with all your heart and lean not to your own understanding."*

God always has the necessary resources when our requirements are exceedingly more than our human resources. God will provide as we put our trust in Him. Another lesson of faith learned; at least until the next test.

Job's faith was also tested and tried when he lost just about everything. The drought he experienced was far more extreme than what I experienced in Kansas. I can't even imagine how he felt through his faith lesson, but God does reward the faithful because God is faithful. Psalm 31:23 says *"The Lord preserves the faithful."* It also says in Psalm 37:28 *"[The Lord] will not forsake His faithful ones."*

The book of Job tells about how Job's resources were lacking but God's resources were abundant. Job lived in the land of Uz. He was blameless and upright; he feared God and shunned evil. He appeared that he was a very wealthy man. He had seven sons and three daughters, and he owned seven thousand sheep, three thousand camels, five hundred yoke of oxen, five hundred donkeys, and had a large number of servants. The Bible says that he was the greatest man among all the people of the East.

One day when the angels came to present themselves before the Lord, Satan also came with them. When the Lord asked where he came from, Satan said, "From roaming through the earth and going back and forth in it." Now, I'm sure at this point you're thinking to yourself, "Doesn't an all-knowing God know where Satan has been?" Of course! God knows everything! But I believe in this instance, God was setting up his plan to test Job. The

Lord answered him, "Have you considered my servant Job? There is not one on earth like him; he is blameless and upright, a man who fears God and shuns evil." Satan answered God, "Does Job fear God for nothing? Have you not put a hedge around him, his household and everything he has? You have blessed the work of his hands, so that his flocks and herds are spread throughout the land. But stretch out your hand and strike everything he has, and he will surely curse you to your face." The Lord then said, "Very well then, everything he has is in your hands, but do not lay a finger on the man himself."

So, Satan went out from the presence of the Lord. In a short period of time, Job's family were attacked and carried off and the servants were killed. Then a fire came down and burned up the sheep and the remaining servants. Then the camels were taken away and a mighty wind swept in from the desert and struck the four corners of the house where his sons and daughters were at, collapsing the house upon them and they died. After all this, Job did not curse God but submitted himself to God and His providence. Job was successful in this first test.

Now comes the second test. This time Satan came before the Lord and said that if Job didn't curse God when everything was taken away from him, he certainly would if the Lord allowed him to touch Job himself. God responded by telling him that he could touch his flesh but his life must be spared. So Satan went out from the Lord's presence and afflicted Job with painful sores from the soles of his feet to the top of his head. Even in all that had happened, Job did not curse God or sin in any way. He passed the second test.

Despite all of Satan's efforts, Job remained faithful to God and God remained faithful to Job. Satan tried many ways, including sending Job's friends to convince him to give up and curse God in order to move Job's faith. Job's faith did not waver and Satan's efforts failed. Job 5:12 says, *"He thwarts the plan of the crafty, so that their hands achieve no success."*

Because of this, God rewarded Job for passing these tests. Job knew that God still reigned supreme over everything and every breath that he breathed was God given. His dominion was eternal and His plan will be accomplished. God is always present and His power unmatched. God would be with him in life and in death.

Because of Job's faithfulness, the Lord rewarded him by making him prosperous again and gave him twice as much as he had before. The Lord blessed the latter part of Job's life more than the first. When we turn to God in times of crisis and testing, He not only sustains us and restores us, but abundantly provides all that we need.

Others may let us down but God will never let us down. God has said in John 26:33, we will have trouble in this world, but He is our refuge in time of trouble. And as we read in Nahum 1:7, *"The Lord is good, a refuge in times of trouble. He cares for those who trust in Him."* No matter how bleak the situation is, God's mighty power is even greater.

I certainly saw this first hand by God's fences of provision when He provided us with clothes, seeds and water. Job certainly saw this first hand when God provided even more that he once had. You can see that first hand too as you trust Him. How big is the God we love and serve? Instead of saying 'can God?' we should really be saying 'God can'. Since we are only human, we are very limited in what we know and see around us. We really can't fully grasp the omnipotent infinite God with our finite minds. The Israelites experienced this when they were caught between the Red Sea and the approaching Egyptians. They didn't see any way out but God had other plans. Psalm 77:19 *"Your road led by a pathway through the sea - a pathway no one knew was there!"* (LB) God's plan is a much better plan and a more perfect plan, than we could ever come up with. The Israelites thought there was no way out but God gave them a miraculous path beyond their imagination to save them. We thought there was no way out of a financial deficit or a major drought but God, through His inexhaustible resources, had His way of showing us that 'GOD CAN'! Our faith in the Lord increased; as well as God's people when they experienced His fences of deliverance from their bondage in Egypt and at the Red Sea. However, faith's lessons come around again at the next crisis and we have to learn it all over again.

God's Word tells us that His light is greater than the deepest darkness, His arms can reach the unreachable, His love goes deeper than the deepest ocean, His forgiveness overpowers sin and His power is beyond measure. This is the God we worship and serve. Now, we just have to learn how to plug into that Holy Righteous power and allow it to permeate into our own lives and through our lives to the world around us. And yet again, this brings us to another lesson of faith and trust. And so, the lesson continues. But in the meantime, Paul's prayer to the Ephesians reminds them and us of God's glorious riches, power and love......

Ephesians 3:16-19: *"I pray that out of His glorious riches He may strengthen you with power through His Spirit in your inner being, so that Christ may dwell in your hearts through faith. And I pray that you, being rooted and established in love, may have power together with all the saints, to grasp how wide and long and high and deep is the love Christ, and to know this love that surpasses knowledge that you may be filled to the measure of all the fullness of God."*

I AM

When at times I feel alone and there's no one I can turn to;
When I'm lost on the road of life, and don't know what to do;
When I feel like a little lamb, a little lamb who strayed
I think of my great Shepherd for He'd find me and He'd say,
"I AM" Jehovah-Shammah "I AM" the God who's there.
When you feel abandoned anyhow or anywhere.
My presence still continues although you cannot see
Beyond the path before you; even through eternity.
"I AM" before creation and through the end of time.
I promise to be faithful until your face meets mine.

When I feel surrounded by the enemy;
When I feel defeated and can't find security;
When there is no shelter to hide where I feel safe
I think of my protector for he'd hide me and he'd say,
"I AM" Jehovah-Nissi "I AM" the God who saves

When you are overwhelmed with life along the way;
My banner covers over you when storms of life come near.
I'll shelter you and I will make the cloudy skies be clear.

When I feel hurt and wounded by pain out of my past;
When scars don't seem to heal and heartaches seem to last;
When I can't see tomorrow through the pain of yesterday;
I'd see the great Physician for He'd touch me and He'd say,
"I AM" Jehovah-Rapha "I AM" the God who heals;
When you face resentment that your heart reveals.
I'll take away your pain and disappointments too.
I will bring you healing; I'll change the old to new.
"I AM" the God who mends your painful broken heart.
I promise to bring comfort for we'll never be apart.

When I feel I've lost all hope and I'm full of despair;
My imperfections let me down, my sins are everywhere.
When my soul finds no relief and on its own be saved
I think of my Redeemer for He'd save me and He'd say,
"I AM" Jehovah-Jireh "I AM" the God who will provide

Salvation for your dying soul through a sacrifice.

The blood of my Son, Jesus, cleansed you from all sin.

I took your soul that once was dead and gave it life again.

"I AM" the God of righteousness; the Savior of your soul.

I promise to forgive you and someday take you home.

No matter what you're going through, all your needs I know.

"I AM" the God who's with you wherever you may go.

"I AM" the God who shelters you amidst the stormy sea.

"I AM" the God who heals your hurts; my love will set you free.

"I AM" the God who will provide forgiveness for your sins, and

Save your soul from certain death to bring you hope again.

"I AM" the God who was, who is and evermore will be;

So put your trust in me alone I'll meet your every need.

I'll hold you in my unseen hand for I am the great "I AM".

@Catherine A. Garrett
February 2000

CHAPTER SEVEN

DESERTS AND RAINFORESTS
(CAN'T STOP A DROUGHT WITH A SPOON OF WATER)

In Kansas there are not any deserts but in the western part of the state there are wide open ranges which can be quite desolate. There you will find ranches, wildlife refuges, grasslands, and the Gypsum Hills also known as the "Kansas Outback". By car, it's a long drive through that area so I can't imagine walking those miles like some of the early settlers did. I'm sure there isn't much water in the Gypsum Hills so it is dependent upon the summer rains or winter snows.

In my lifetime, I've seen years of plenty and years of want; mostly want. I've seen years of an overabundance of rain and years of never-ending drought. Farming depends on water for growing crops, watering animals and replenishing the water supply in the creeks and cisterns for those who live there. Water is an important element to any land. It is a life-source to man and animals. Many people have taken others to court over water rights and have even gone to war over water. When there's plenty of water, all is good but when there's not, many suffer. As mentioned in the previous chapter, drought hit Kansas while we lived there and many indeed suffered including our family.

God uses many situations, including a time of drought, to bring about His plan and glory; one of which was the story about a seventeen old young man named Joseph. Genesis 37 tells us that Joseph was one of Jacob's eleven sons. Those who have siblings know the relationship can bring competition, sometimes contention and even jealousy between them. Joseph and his brothers were no different. Since Joseph was Jacob's youngest and born of his old age, Jacob loved Joseph more than any of his children and made a richly ornamented colorful robe for him. Their father's partiality and exceptional expression of honor toward Joseph, made his brothers very jealous and envious and they hated him. In fact, they could not speak a kind word to him (Genesis 37:4). Our partiality toward others causes strife and broken relationships. God's Word says, *"The Lord our God does not tolerate injustice, partiality or corruption."* 2 Chronicles 19:7. In fact, according to James 2:9, showing partiality is a sin. Remember, Jacob, as well as all of us were born with a sin nature but God will forgive us when we humbly seek His forgiveness.

Because Joseph believed that God was faithful and he was faithful to Him, God blessed him with the gift of prophetic dreams and interpretation. He shared two of these dreams with his brothers and father. In one of the dreams, Joseph and his brothers were binding their sheaves of grain out in the field when suddenly Joseph's sheaf rose and stood upright and his brothers' sheaves gathered around his and bowed down to it. In the other dream, the sun, moon and eleven stars were bowing down to him. Although at the time, Joseph didn't understand them or were able to interpret these prophetic dreams, His brothers were angered and jealous of him, but his father kept the matter in mind. The truth of these dreams would certainly be revealed later.

The story tells us that Joseph's brothers were grazing the sheep near Shechem when his father sent him to see if everything was well with them and the flocks and to bring word back to him. But Joseph found them in Dothan rather than Shechem.

When they saw Joseph coming at a distance, because of their jealousy, they plotted to get rid of him. Some of the brothers decided to kill him and make it seem like a wild animal had killed him on the way there. But his brother Rueben convinced them not to shed any blood but instead, throw him into a cistern so he could secretly rescue him later and take him back to his father. So the brothers took him, stripped him from his elegant robe and threw him into a waterless cistern. As they sat down to eat their meal, they looked up and saw a caravan of Ishmaelites coming from Gilead with camels loaded up with spices, balm and myrrh which they were taking on their way to Egypt. So they decided that rather to kill him and cover up his blood, they would sell him to these traders. They sold him for twenty shekels of silver to the Midianite merchants who took Joseph to Egypt.

While in Egypt, Joseph went through many stages of struggles but God blessed him nonetheless. In fact, whatever Joseph did he prospered. I'm sure there were many times that he was discouraged and felt abandoned by his brothers and by God. But God had a plan. If being an Egyptian slave wasn't bad enough, Joseph was falsely accused of a crime because of a lie by Potiphar's wife and thrown into the Egyptian prison. While there, God used dreams and gave him a true interpretation of those dreams to bring him directly in front of the Pharaoh of Egypt to interpret his dreams. God gave Joseph the meaning of Pharaoh's dream by revealing that there were to be seven years of plenty and seven years of drought. Because Joseph interpreted Pharaoh's dream and provided a plan to save them from the coming drought, Joseph was placed in charge of the whole land of Egypt.

During the second year of the drought, Joseph would have been about forty years old. Because of the drought, people from all the surrounding nations came to Egypt to buy grain. One of those people were his ten brothers, except Benjamin who was the youngest who stayed with his father Jacob. Joseph recognized his brothers but they didn't recognize him. To test them to see if they had changed throughout the years, he accused them of being spies just as they had accused Joseph of years earlier when he reported to his father of his brothers bad behavior. They replied to his accusations by telling Joseph that there once were twelve brothers, one was left with their father and one was no more. Despite their continual insistence that they weren't spies, Joseph ordered one of the brothers stay in Egypt while they go and bring back the other brother to prove what they are saying and in turn prove that they weren't spies. So he took Simeon, placed him in prison and sent the other brothers back to their father, along with grain, as well as the silver that they brought to pay for the grain.

Once they returned to their father, they explained that they must return to Egypt with Benjamin in order to free Simeon from prison and prove that they weren't spies. When they arrived back in Egypt, Joseph saw that his brothers still hadn't changed so he tested them once again. Once they finished feasting and drinking with Joseph, they were allowed to leave with donkeys full of bags of grain but he had his servants place his silver cup in the mouth of the bag which was loaded onto Benjamin's donkey. They were stopped on the way out of the city and were accused of taking the cup. When they searched for it, it was found in Benjamin's bag. They were brought again before Joseph and were adamant that Benjamin didn't take it but Joseph persisted he did because it was found in his bag. The brothers didn't have any explanation but conceded that because of this sin against Joseph, that they would be his slaves. But Joseph told them that since it was in Benjamin's bag, that he would stay and become his slave and that all the others were free to leave. However, since they knew how it would hurt their father, they said that the boy cannot leave his father because if he leaves him, his father will die. They explained that if he is taken him from his father just as the other brother was taken away from him (speaking about Joseph), it will bring his gray hair down to the grave in misery and sorrow. That showed Joseph that his brothers were now concerned about his brother Benjamin and the loss that their father would experience if Benjamin couldn't return to him. Joseph saw that their hearts had now changed. He then revealed himself to his brothers, but his brothers were unable to answer because they were terrified that Joseph would punish them for what they had done.

What Joseph said next would show that his brothers' plan could not thwart God's plan. Joseph told them in Genesis 45: 4 -8 *"I am your brother Joseph, the one you sold into Egypt! And now, do not be distressed and do not be angry with yourselves for selling me here, because it was to save lives that God sent me ahead of you. For two years now there has been famine in the land, and for the next five years there will not be plowing or reaping. But God sent me ahead of you to preserve for you a remnant on earth and to save lives by a great deliverance. So then, it was not you who sent me here, but God. He made me father to Pharaoh, lord of his entire household and ruler of all Egypt."*

Despite all that Joseph went through during those years in Egypt, God used drought to restore his relationship with his brothers and father. Sometimes God uses droughts in our lives as well, to restore our earthly relationships and our relationship with God.

Drought can come in many forms. It can be a rain drought, a financial drought, a relationship drought, an emotional drought, and even a spiritual drought. During my lifetime, I've experienced all of these; mostly because I'm human and I still live here in an imperfect world.

Like many of us, Joseph had to experience waiting on God. He had to wait for many years for God's will and plan to come into fruition. When we would plant crops in the fields, we had to wait until we saw any sign of the plants shooting through the ground. In our life journey, there are many times that we are waiting on God to move.

Sometimes we get anxious and move ahead of God but God's word says that we are to be patient with His fences of waiting. Psalm 46:10 says *"Be still and know that I am God."* We are to wait expectantly knowing our seeds will yield crops in its time and God will work in His time. This is expressed in Isaiah 49:23 *"Those who hope in me will not be disappointed."* Although Joseph had to go through many trials and a lot of waiting when he was in Egypt, he certainly was not disappointed when he was reunited with his father once again. We need to remember, God's timing is perfect because He is perfect.

In chapter six, I've already recounted how, through God's miraculous intervention, our garden flourished beyond our human expectation, even in the midst of a major drought, as well as how He brought much needed rain after working tirelessly to water it ourselves.

In addition to all of our human efforts, we chose to trust in God to provide. In that situation, our faith was stronger than our fear of drought. God promises that when we trust in the Lord, we will have confidence in Him. The prophet Jeremiah, goes into detail regarding this.

Jeremiah 17: 7 and 8 says, *"But blessed is the man who trusts in the Lord, whose confidence is in Him. He will be like a tree planted by the water that sends out its roots by the stream. It does not fear when heat comes, its leaves are always green. It has no worries in a year of drought and never fails to bear fruit."*

Unfortunately it seems that many forms of drought continue and there's another lesson of faith to learn.

Personally, learning to have faith while facing financial drought seems to be the most difficult and to be honest, sometimes downright impossible. I know what you're thinking – nothing is impossible with God (Luke 1:37). I read and reread that verse over and over and should have it tattooed on my forehead by now so I can remember this promise the next time I need faith to get me through my next test.

During the year of drought, my pregnancy, and my husband's disability, we conserved as much as we could with a three year old and one on the way, but it never seemed enough to keep a roof over our heads, clothes on our backs, utilities on, our car in good working order and food on the table. The garden certainly helped. We ran out of a lot of things but we certainly didn't run out of green beans. During that time, neither did we run out of faith in God's provisions. In that year, we passed the test.

Like so many out there in today's world, struggling with financial drought is a constant battle. With every new battle, I constantly pray that my Heavenly Father will get me out of it. Maybe I'm asking for the wrong thing. Maybe I should be asking Him to help me through it instead of out of it. I have come to the conclusion that not everything here on earth is fixable. Well, no duh! We are a broken and sinful people living in a broken and sinful world. Knowing this, I can rest assured that in God's time, everything will be fixed here on Earth as well as in Heaven. There are more people currently now in debt than in any other time in history. Not only individually but nationally. Until I leave this earth, I am sure I will always struggle with financial drought, but the real question is will I have enough faith in God's fences of provision to get me through it? I guess time will tell if I will pass or fail that next lesson.

Spiritual drought is quite difficult too. Mainly because you don't know you are in it until you are deep in it. First, you stop reading God's Word, then the prayer life dwindles and then you stop going to church. I find that when I am in that place of complacency, my life around me doesn't seem to go as well. Although God's presence is always with me as God has promised, it's like I lose touch with not only God but I lose touch with my soul and the Holy Spirit. As I've heard said, I'm the one who moved; not God.

Proverbs warns us of this in 1:29-33 *"Since they would not accept my advice and spurned my rebuke, they will eat the fruit of their ways and be filled with the fruit of their schemes. For the waywardness of the simple will kill them, and the complacency of fools will destroy them; but whoever listens to me will live in safety and be at ease, without fear of harm."* The Bible also calls this "lukewarm". It is being self-satisfied, self-sufficient and content in what you have and take no regard of what God has given. In the book of Revelation, God describes the people of Laodicea lukewarm by saying in Revelation 3:15 through 17: *"I know your deeds, that you are neither cold nor hot. I wish you were one or the other! So, because you are lukewarm – neither hot or cold – I am about to spit you out of my mouth. You say, I am rich; I have acquired wealth and do not need a thing. But you do not realize that you are wretched, pitiful, poor, blind and naked."* The people of Laodicea stopped trusting in God and started trusting in themselves. They left God out of the equation, like many of us do sometimes too.

Throughout the droughts and deserts of life, keeping daily connected to God through the Holy Spirit will keep us in tune with God and in turn will prevent us from becoming lukewarm. Unfortunately, the Israelites learned this lesson the hard way when they left Egypt and entered their desert journey.

At the end of 430 years of enduring slavery in Egypt, Moses began to lead the Israelites out of Egypt towards the land that God had promised. But it wasn't going to be easy. They had to cross many miles of desert to get there. Not only did they have the distance to overcome, but their hearts also had to be ready and in tune with God's heart before they could enter into their Promised Land.

Their first test was when the Egyptians had them cornered at the Red Sea. God's purposes are always right and it was God's purpose to direct Moses to place them there to again see His power. When the Israelites saw the Egyptians approaching, they became terrified. Exodus 14:11 and 12 shows that their fear was greater than their faith. *"They said to Moses, 'Was it because there were no graves in Egypt that you brought us to the desert to die? What have you done to us by bringing us out of Egypt? Didn't we say to you in Egypt 'Leave us alone; let us serve the Egyptians'? It would have been better for us to serve the Egyptians than to die in the desert!'"* First of all, they were accusing Moses of bringing this upon them but Moses didn't bring them there. God did. Secondly, they said they should have remained as slaves in Egypt but they cried to God for 430 years to rescue them from slavery. Thirdly, they weren't even in the wilderness yet but was only a few days walk. Yet, they were already grumbling about their situation and forgot all of the miracles that God's mighty hand performed back in Egypt to deliver them from bondage. Moses told them not to be afraid, stand firm and they will see the deliverance of the Lord; the Lord will fight for them. We all know that God did deliver them (again) by parting the waters. They walked over on dry ground and the Egyptians died when they tried to follow. The Israelites failed their first test to depend on God rather than on their own resources in that circumstance. There were many more tests to come during their journey.

Deserts are harsh environments with little food or water. The people started grumbling (again) for water and food. In those instances through God's fences of direction and provision, Moses threw a piece of wood into the bitter waters at Marah and they became sweet. God provided them water to drink. Then the people grumbled at Moses again; this time for food. They told Moses that they had plenty of food in Egypt and accused him again of bringing them out to the desert to die. So the Lord rained down bread from Heaven called Manna. Moses described it as being white like coriander seed and tasted like wafers of honey. He gave them instructions on how much they could gather each day as a test to see if they would follow His directions. But they didn't listen, so some of the Manna developed maggots and began to smell. Then the Israelites became tired of Manna and wanted something else to eat so God provided quail. They again complained to Moses about water to drink, so God directed Moses to strike a rock and when he did, water came forth.

    They were never satisfied with anything that the Lord gave them and longed for the richness of Egypt. Again, they failed the test of relying on God instead of their own devices. Do we do that? Do I do that? Do I fail to rely on God's richness and His fence of provision during the droughts of my life? There have been times I have not but there has been times that I have, but unfortunately, it never seems to be a consistent faith. Sometimes I just get wrapped up in my situation by trying to solve it myself with only human resources; I forget to turn to God, who has eternal resources. We are stubborn and selfish but God is loving and patient. He wants us to trust Him in every part of our lives and is longing for us to go to Him with our every need. It only takes a small step of faith for God to move in a very large way.

    The Israelites and I have both discovered that our fear is small compared to God's greatness and power. God is bigger than all of our fears combined. The trouble is, we sometimes forget that. My husband preached a sermon called "God Can!" He emphasized that a lot of times we say "Can God?" instead of "God Can!" because our fears overcome our faith in God. This same thing happened when the Israelites were facing the Philistines and a very huge guy named Goliath, who was a champion among them. According to I Samuel 17, Goliath was over nine feet tall, had a bronze helmet on his head, wore a coat of armor of bronze weighing two hundred pounds, leg shields, and carried a javelin with an iron spearhead weighing twenty five pounds. Seeing this, all the Israelites were trembling with fear when Goliath was taunting someone to fight him. And after continuing his taunting for forty days, some were running away with fright. I'm pretty sure I would too! Then a young shepherd boy named David, stood up among all the fearful Israelites and said in I Samuel 17, verses 26b and 32 *"Who is this heathen Philistine anyway, that he is allowed to defy the armies of the living God? Let no one lose heart on account of this Philistine; your servant will go and fight him."* But when everyone said that he couldn't do it, David told them that while watching his father's sheep, he killed a lion and a bear and with God's help, he rescued them. So surely, if the Lord delivered him from the lion and the bear, He will certainly deliver him from the hand of this Philistine. The Israelites saw a big Goliath but David saw a bigger God. David, armed only with five smooth stones in his shepherd's bag, his shepherd's staff and sling, walked out to face Goliath. David wasn't saying "Can God?" but he was saying "God Can!" And God did! It only took one of the five stones to hit Goliath right in the middle of the forehead to knock him to the ground. It may have been David's full confidence in God's fence of protection but I have no doubt that God directed that stone as it flew through the air to land at the perfect spot where there was no armor. Because of this victory, the Philistines ran in fear of Israel's God. David proclaimed before the Philistines in I Samuel 17:45, 47 *"You come against me with sword and spear and javelin, but I come against you in the name of the Lord Almighty, the God of the armies of*

Israel, who you have defied. All those gathered here will know that it is not by sword or spear that the Lord saves; before the battle is the Lord's, and He will give all of you into our hands."

Psalm 18:30-32 *"As for God, His way is perfect; the word of God is flawless. He is a shield for all who take refuge in Him. For who is God besides the Lord? And who is the Rock besides our God? It is God who arms me with strength and makes my way perfect."*

Psalm 18:37-40 *"I pursued my enemies and overtook them; I did not turn back till they were destroyed. I crushed them so that they could not rise; they fell beneath my feet. You armed me with strength for the battle; you made my adversaries bow at my feet. You made my enemies turn their backs in flight, and I destroyed my foes."*

  Oh, I'd love to have as much faith as David when I'm faced with the giants in my life; like financial debt, when my car needs replacing, when my garden needs watering during a drought, when my husband passes away, when I retire. The funny thing is, looking back, it seems that God tested my faith in small steps and gave me time to learn faith little by little before He gave me bigger tests. I'm thankful that He is bigger than my failures and His patience is consistent during all of my struggles of faith.

II Timothy 2:3 *"Even when we are too weak to have any faith left, He remains faithful to us and will help us, for He cannot disown us who are part of Himself, and He will always carry out His promises to us."* (LB)

CHAPTER EIGHT

LIFE AND DEATH

(THE HOUR GLASS OF HUMANITY)

If you've lived long enough, at some time or another, you've had to experience the death of a family member, a spouse, or friend. I have seen the burial of both grandparents on my mother's side and my father's side. My mother passed when I was fifteen years old at age forty seven of cancer. My father passed years later when I was thirty nine years old at age seventy six. I've also seen many friends and acquaintances pass from life to death. Depending on whether they were a believer or not, there are different reactions to those left behind.

When we go through life, we always believe that our loved ones, friends and even ourselves, will continue living forever on this earth, but realistically we know that death is inevitable because that's just part of life. I certainly didn't expect that my mother would die when I was so young. I thought she and my dad would always be there. I'm sure there are many who are reading this whose mom or dad are still living think that too. But we don't know when our day of reckoning will come when we will face God, our maker. The Bible says our days are numbered and God knows that number. God ordained those days before we were even born. Psalm 139:16b *"All the days ordained for me were written in your book before one of them came to be."* God's Word also tells us that whether we will live to be forty seven, seventy six or one hundred, we're here one day, gone the next. No matter if we feel we're invincible, our life here on earth is really a very short journey.

      When our family lived on the farm, my maternal grandparents lived in town. My grandmother had the greenest thumb; of which I unfortunately did not inherit. She could grow anything and I actually think she did. Her whole front yard was like an arboretum filled with many different seasonal flowers, bushes and trees. East of the house the spring flowers would pop up which would include crocus and many different colored irises and poppies. One of my favorites were the poppies because of their large array of colors and how delicate they were. But because of their delicate nature, they only lasted a little while. Once the wind came up, their pedals would start falling off one by one until they were completely stripped of color. I was so disappointed because I then had to wait until the next spring to see them again. That's how we as humans are. Here one moment and in a blink of an eye, gone the next. We are only here showing our colors for such a very short time compared to the viewpoint of eternity. Psalm 103:15-16 says *"As for man, his days are like grass, he flourishes like a flower in the field; the wind blows over it and it is gone, and its place remembers it no more."* And Psalm 89:48 says *"What man can live and not see death, or save himself from the grave?"*

      Death is such a bleak topic to talk about and in fact, some people want to ignore the subject altogether. Most people live their lives with the belief that they will live forever but death is inevitable. I'm sure Lazarus didn't give it much thought himself until he experienced death in a most unique and miraculous way.

It was a day like any other day in Bethany where Lazarus and his sisters Mary and Martha lived. They were busy with their everyday routine and had no idea that the next day would bring so much sorrow. When Lazarus returned home that day, he was feverish and didn't feel well. He laid down and his sisters immediately tended to him with the hope of a quick recovery. Seeing that his recovery didn't come, they sent word to Jesus saying, "Lord, the one you love is sick." Unfortunately, Lazarus died before Jesus arrived.

When their message arrived to where Jesus was, Jesus said in John 11:4 *"This sickness will not end in death. No, it is for God's glory so that God's Son may be glorified through it."* Jesus loved Lazarus as well as his sisters Mary and Martha but even knowing his friend Lazarus is sick, He stayed where He was for two more days. After then, He told His disciples that they were going back to Judea saying that our friend has fallen asleep but He was going to wake him up.

When Martha heard of Jesus' arrival at Bethany, she ran to Him saying if He had been there her brother would not have died. But Jesus responded to her in John 11:25-26 *"I am the resurrection and the life. He who believes in me will live, even though he dies, and whoever lives and believes in me will never die."* At that point, I'm sure she didn't quite understand what he said but Jesus certainly wasn't done yet. Despite the fact that Lazarus had been dead for three days, Jesus tells them to remove the stone. He calls Lazarus to come out and indeed, Lazarus comes back to life again before the amazed crowd of onlookers. I can guarantee that a miracle of raising someone from the dead spread everywhere like wild fire and would have certainly been front page news today! But the biggest question is how did it effect those watching first hand that day; His disciples, Mary, Martha and especially Lazarus? According to the records, Lazarus was about thirty years old when Jesus raised him to life and lived another thirty years after that took place.

Being only thirty years old, I would guess that Lazarus didn't think much about death but I'm sure that after that, he thought a lot about life. Because of Jesus, he had another thirty years of life with his sisters and he most assuredly used it for God's glory.

Sometimes it takes us facing death to get a better and richer perspective of life. We think differently how we've lived our lives here on earth and how God wants to make it richer and more meaningful going forward. Death also gives us pause about life after death and where we would want to spend eternity. If you are a believer in the Lord Jesus Christ as I am, we are practicing for Heaven while we are still here on earth. We don't know when God will call us home but when that time comes, we want to make sure we've done everything He has asked us to do and to learn every lesson we need to learn. Until that time, we should strive to continue to pass God's love and salvation to those who will remain.

In 1986, while on his way to work one morning, my husband was involved in a very bad rear-end collision. He was sitting at a red light when a fully loaded semi-tractor trailer hit him at full speed. The impact was so hard that it threw items from the front seat into the back seat, broke his driver's seat and left him with a herniated disc. After an unsuccessful back surgery, he was left in a semi-bed ridden state with severe pain, nerve damage and was no longer able to work. At times, he was able to get up and start dinner for me before I returned home from work or take the kids to basketball practice but for the most part, he laid on his hospital bed at home for the remainder of his life.

There were many obstacles to climb during that time; financial, emotional, relational and spiritual. Our family was struggling with all of it. That semi-truck not only destroyed our car but it also destroyed our way of life. Before 1986, our family always listened to God and tried to live a life worthy of God's calling. We strived to raise our children to love the Lord so that they would walk with Him all the days of their lives. My husband pastored a church back in Kansas for a year and half while attending Bible College. We taught Vacation Bible School together and we also taught Sunday school classes. My husband's strength and faith in the Lord was always my strength and faith but after the accident, I could no longer see him with that same strength and faith. We started to crumble; I started to crumble. We all were losing ground in every way possible and about to fall over the edge of the cliff when something happened even more devastating that certainly wasn't expected or in the horizon.

In February 1993, my husband started coughing. At first, thinking it was just a chest cold but because of his stubbornness, he didn't want to go to a doctor. But the coughing continued and became more frequently severe. Since I've had bronchitis and pneumonia before and knew the symptoms, I thought he should go to the doctor to see if that might be the issue. Early March I finally got him to go and sure enough, the doctor's diagnosis was bronchitis. He was sent home with some medicine but it didn't seem to resolve the issue and in fact, within weeks, it had become even more severe. By early April, it sounded like pneumonia. I was trying to talk him into going back to the doctor when I got a call that I've been dreading the most.

My sister called me to tell me that our dad, who lives in Kansas, was in the hospital and wasn't expected to live. What? Weren't I going through enough already? How can this be happening? I even remember asking again how a loving God do this to me. My husband was really sick, I had three children at home that needed me and now my dad was dying. I had no choice. If I wanted to see my dad alive, I had to go. I couldn't get a flight out on Saturday, April third so I ended up flying out on Sunday, April fourth. My husband and two of my children drove me to the airport. On the way, I made my husband promise me that once he dropped me off, he would go to the doctor. With the assurance that he would, I flew out.

After they dropped me off, my husband decided not go to the doctor as he promised but started to head home. My daughter demanded that he go since he promised me so they headed to the doctors. When my husband walked into the doctor's office he immediately collapsed. They don't even know how he drove himself there because he only had five percent oxygen left in his body. They immediately admitted him to the ICU and was placed on a ventilator.

    Meanwhile back in Kansas, my sister picked me up at the airport and we immediately went to the hospital to see our dad. I and my three sisters were gathered around dad's bed. He was having a hard time breathing but I could tell he was so happy to see us all there; surrounded by his girls. We had a great visit and before I left the hospital, I decided to call home to see how my husband was feeling and what the doctor said. My daughter answered the phone but I could immediately tell by her voice that she was anxious and worried. She told me that she was so glad I called because her dad, my husband, was in the hospital. I wasn't too worried because I thought he just had pneumonia but asked if the doctor knew what was wrong with him but she said they didn't have a diagnosis yet. I told her that I would call the hospital before I left to go to my sister's house. As soon as I hung up, I called and spoke to the nurse on duty. She said he was sedated in ICU and they didn't know what's wrong with him at that time. That news made me more concerned and worried but I went on to my sister's house to spend the night with the plan to come back the next day to see my dad again.

    That night, we all were getting into bed when the phone rang. On the other end of the phone was the night nurse at the hospital where my husband was at. She said they still didn't know what was wrong yet but she strongly suggested that I needed to get back there. I couldn't believe it. My dad was near death lying in the hospital in Kansas and my husband was near death in a hospital in California. I was torn but I knew what I had to do. I had to get back to California to be with my husband and children. But I wanted to see my dad one last time.

We got back to the hospital early the next day so I could say goodbye to my dad, because that was the last time I'd see him alive. My heart held such sorrow; it felt like my heart was being torn asunder. I told my dad that my husband was in the hospital and I had to return to California. He understood. My eyes filled with tears as I walked out of that room. The word heartbreak couldn't describe how I was feeling. That was the hardest thing that I've ever done. At least that's what I thought at the time but I would soon find out later that it wouldn't be.

I cried all the way back on the plane. I couldn't be consoled. My husband's uncle picked me up at the airport and drove me directly to the hospital where my husband laid sedated in ICU. When I walked into his room and spoke to him, it looked like he moved his lips. He was probably saying to me "Why aren't you with your dad?" because he knew how much my dad's condition was worrying me.

The next morning, I received a call from my sister to let me know that my dad had passed away during the night. Although I knew it was coming, I was still broken up about it. My husband passed away five days later. The month of April was a hard month for sure. It sounds odd but I was angry at my husband because I thought he could have fought harder. I was also angry and very disappointed because I couldn't go back to Kansas for my dad's military funeral. I had to stay where I was to bury a husband. This isn't the way it was supposed to be. I was now a widow with three young children. I found myself even angry at God for letting all this happen. All I could do is pray "God help me!"

One day not too long after that, I was pondering and praying about what had just happened. I was trying to figure out how I was going to live without a husband, who had been my strength for years. I relied on him; physically and spiritually. Yes, he was disabled but he was a very large man standing six feet six inches. He was strong and I knew that if someone was trying to hurt me or his family that he would go in like a roaring rhino to protect us. He was also our family's spiritual leader. At that moment, God spoke to me as an audible voice in my heart and mind. He gave me the following comforting verse in Isaiah 54: 4-5 *"Do not be afraid; you will not suffer shame. Do not fear disgrace; you will not be humiliated. You will forget the shame of your youth and remember no more the reproach of your widowhood. For your Maker is your husband – the Lord Almighty is His name – the Holy One of Israel is your Redeemer; He is called the God of all the earth."* The Lord was reassuring me that although I lost my earthly husband, He, himself would now be my husband. God put all that I physically went through into a spiritual perspective. He was my strength; not my husband. At that point, I knew I could live the rest of my life here on earth at peace knowing God would always be by my side, even if my husband wasn't.

Just as life has a large effect on us, so does death. For most people, facing death can profoundly change the way people look at life. Sometimes death of a loved one or close friend makes us angry and sometimes even abandoned. Since I lost my mom to cancer when I was young, I felt like when my dad passed away I would feel like an orphan and in a strange way, abandoned here on earth since both of my parents were gone. Then when it actually happened, those feelings had to be set aside because of what was going on with my husband. I didn't even have to deal with those feelings after all, because my emotional state was overridden by my husband's condition and subsequent death. It is kind of odd how those pre-emptive feelings didn't even matter anymore. God took care of that too!

Through these events, God has taught me that He will never leave me or forsake me, even if I live to be a hundred years old. And when it's my time for me to leave this earth and go home to Heaven, God will be by my side then too. It says in Psalm 139:7-8, *"Where can I go from your Spirit? Where can I flee from your presence? If I go up in the heavens, you are there; if I make my bed in the depth, you are there."* No matter where I am or where you are, God's presence is with us.

God's Word says that death is inevitable in Psalm 89:48 *"What man can live and not see death, or save himself from the power of the grave?"* So if that's the truth of the matter, how shall we live? God's Word also gives us some teachable truths on how to live in the face of death. In Psalm 90:12, David says *"Teach us to number our days aright, that we may gain a heart of wisdom."* In other words, appreciate each day and seek God for wisdom. We shouldn't take our days for granted because there's no guarantee of our next breath, let alone the next day.

There are many other Biblical references that show us how God wants to live. Among them are a list of God's requirements in Micah 6:8 – *"To act justly, and to love mercy and to walk humbly with your God."* Also in Galatians 6:9 – *"Let us not become weary in doing good, for at the proper time we will reap a harvest if we do not give up."* Also in Galatians is listed the Fruits of the Spirit: *"Love, peace, patience, kindness, goodness, faithfulness, gentleness and self-control."* The Apostle Paul encourages us in Romans 12:18 *"If it is possible, as far as it depends on you, live at peace with everyone."* There are many strands of life that God's Word touches on but there is always one I struggle with in Galatians 3:11 *"…The righteous will live by faith."* And that brings us back around to what this book is about….Faith. Faith in the face of life. Faith in the face of death. Faith in the face of uncertainty. Faith in the face of painful circumstances. Faith in God's fences of providence, grace, comfort and love.

All we have to do is to have faith in our Heavenly Father who can see around the corner and far into eternity; even before we take our next breath. Having faith in an inheritance in Heaven is the easy part, but having faith in the here and now, as well as for the future while on Earth, is the hard part. And so, the lesson of faith continues.

Matthew 6:31-34 *"So do not worry, saying, 'What shall we eat?' or 'What shall we drink?' or 'What shall we wear?' For the pagans run after all these things, and your Heavenly Father knows that you need them. But seek first His Kingdom and His Righteousness, and all these things will be given to you as well. Therefore do not worry about tomorrow, for tomorrow will worry about itself. Each day has enough trouble of its own."*

Philippians 4:19 *"And my God will meet all your needs according to His glorious riches in Christ Jesus."*

CHAPTER NINE

MY FATHER'S LEGACY

(GOD'S PROMISED INHERITANCE)

My father was tall and slender, very kind, gentle, had good strong morals, and a man of little words. When he did speak, it was something important. He never really liked crowds but yet, everyone who knew him, liked him. As I mentioned before, to me he seemed to be the strongest man in the whole world. He spent a few years in the U.S. Army, which was the reason I thought it was surprising that he didn't like fighting; especially between me and my sisters. Although on occasion I and my sisters annoyed each other, I don't remember that we fought that much. Where would we find the time anyway? We had a farm to take care of and chores to do. We had forty acres of fencing to mend, cows to milk, chickens and ducks to feed, gardens to tend, as well as household chores. On top of that, there was planting and harvesting; as well as relocating the hay bales from the field into the barn.

Every Sunday, we would attend our local church. I only remember one Sunday when we couldn't get there because of a major snow storm. Other than that, we never missed. Both of my parents loved the Lord and lived out that love to others. One time a homeless man came to our farm porch door asking for food, as we were sitting down for supper, which my parents gladly shared. I can still see my mom, with her memorable big smile, generously handing the man the plate of food on the front step and how full of gratitude the man was.

    I am blessed to have grown up in a very quiet, respectful and Godly home. Because I grew up with an earthly father who had a gentle, peaceful and loving spirit, I saw my Heavenly father in the same way. In comparison, my view of my earthly father was based on how I saw my Heavenly Father. It was like my Heavenly Father was a magnification of my earthly father. But for those who had an earthly father who was abusive, mean-spirited and exhibited no grace in the raising of his children, often look at the Heavenly Father that same way too. I've known many people who experienced one of these two scenarios. For those who grew up in grace were certainly blessed, but those who grew up in judgement and think God is the same way, need to look closer at the Heavenly Father's attributes.

    Many of God's attributes are threaded throughout the pages of the Bible, but here are just a few.

<u>Compassionate and loving</u>

    Psalm 103: 8 *"The Lord is compassionate and gracious, slow to anger, abounding in love."*

<u>Faithful</u>

    Psalm 145:13 *"The Lord is faithful to all his promises and loving toward all He has made."*

<u>Accessible</u>

Psalm 27:10 *"Though my father and mother forsake me, the Lord will receive me."*

Patient

II Peter 3:9 *"He [God] is patient with you, not wanting anyone to perish, but everyone to come to repentance."*

Merciful

Titus 3:4 and 5 *"But when the kindness and love of God our Savior appeared, He saved us, not because of righteous things we had done, but because of His mercy."*

Forgiving

I John 1:9 *"If we confess our sins, He is faithful and just and will forgive us our sins and purify us from all unrighteousness."*

My dad exhibited good God-given character and strong values. I saw these traits in the way he lived; not only in our family circle but also toward others. These added value to his legacy for all generations that followed. I believe that God's work within him resulted in an eternal legacy for me personally and I in turn, hope to do the same for generations that follow me. The question is, will I leave a positive or a negative legacy? That's an important question for all of us to ask.

Good character and positive relationships can go a long way. These can turn a heart and soul away from a negative situation or environment onto a positive path. Jesus brought light to the world for thirty three years. He taught those he encountered to turn the other cheek, to help others and show love and compassion. Two examples involved two Samaritans. Samaritans were a mixed race who worshipped other gods and did not follow Jewish customs and rituals, which caused the Jews to despise them. This caused hostility between them.

One of these examples was shown in the parable of the Good Samaritan, which Jesus told in Luke, chapter 10. In this parable, Jesus told about a man who was traveling from Jerusalem to Jericho when he was robbed, stripped of his clothing, beaten and left for dead on the side of the road. A Jewish priest came by, saw the man, but passed by on the other side of the road. Then a Levite came by and saw him but also passed by on the other side. Neither men had any compassion on the injured man. The Bible doesn't tell us whether the man was Jewish or of another nationality but they certainly pronounced judgment or just didn't care enough to get involved. The legacy left for their children would not have been very noble, loving or merciful, but of hearts full of judgment and intolerance.

Then a Samaritan came by, saw the man and took pity on him. He bandaged his wounds, put him on his donkey and took him to an innkeeper. He instructed the innkeeper to look after the man, handed him two silver coins and told him that when he returns, he will reimburse any extra expenses incurred while he was away. What kind of legacy did the Samaritan leave his family? The legacy that this Samaritan left to his family was a legacy of love, mercy and sympathy towards others who are in need. He was certainly a better neighbor than the priest or the Levite. His positive actions were a testament to his character and would have been reflected in what he taught his descendants. His kindness toward someone in need and his compassion is a legacy that would have been a positive one for generations to come, even after he had died.

Another example of an eternal legacy resulted from a not-so-random encounter of Jesus with a Samaritan woman. Considering the hostility between the Jews and Samaritans, it is surprising that Jesus would interact at all with a Samaritan. I'm sure she was even more surprised that a Jew would speak to a Samaritan. The book of John tells us that when Jesus and his disciples were heading back to Galilee, they had to go through Samaria. John says that Jesus, tired from his journey, sat down by Jacob's well to rest while his disciples had gone into town to buy food. While He was sitting there, a Samaritan woman came to the well to draw water. Jesus asked if she would give him a drink from the well. Since Jews don't associate with Samaritans, she was surprised because Jesus was a Jew and she was a Samaritan woman. Jesus then responded to her in John 4:10 *"If you knew the gift of God and who it is that asks for a drink, you would have asked him and he would have given you living water."* Of course, she was still thinking that He was talking about literal water, but Jesus quickly clarifies that in John 4:13 *"Everyone who drinks this water will be thirsty again, but whoever drinks the water I give him will never thirst. Indeed, the water I give him will become him a spring of water welling up to eternal life."* I am sure that surprised her as much as it would have surprised us as well but she quickly responded that she wanted that water so she wouldn't be thirsty again. After a few more minutes of conversation, Jesus identifies Himself as the Messiah. Now that must have completely caught her off guard but she was so excited that she went immediately into town and told everyone she could find. Because of that personal revelation by that Samaritan women's encounter with Christ and her testimony, many Samaritans believed. The legacy she left was salvation to many generations.

    We just never know how are words or actions will have a lasting effect on those generations that follow. One day Jesus was teaching in Capernaum. There were so many who gathered to hear Him that there wasn't any more room, not even outside the door. While Jesus was preaching the Word to them, four men came carrying a paralytic man on a mat but they couldn't even get close to Jesus. So they made an opening in the roof above Jesus and lowered the mat which the paralytic was lying on. Through these four men and their persistence and faith in Jesus, their friend was healed that day; not only physically but also spiritually. What kind of men were these that did that for a friend? What kind of legacy will they leave? Kindness. Faith. Brotherhood. Compassion. Love. This legacy was not only left to the one who was healed but also for those who saw their compassion and faith that day.

    Hand-me-downs were common to our farm life. My parents couldn't afford new clothing and shoes so sometimes we wore hand-me-downs. I wore my older sister's clothing; at least until I outgrew her. My younger sister wore hand-me-downs from me and my older sister. But generation to generation hand-me-downs may not just pertain to clothing or property, but it could also pertain to Godly character, moral and ethical strength and positive attributes and traits. We all have seen how positive and negative character can influence our families and the world around us. Good positive character provides positive results but negative character provides negative results. Paul puts this in perspective in his letter to the Corinthians.

I Corinthians 15:33 *"Do not be misled; bad company corrupts good character."*

My family was poor and we worked hard for everything we had. Farming wasn't very glorious like other jobs but on the flip side, it taught me appreciation for everything. We eventually had to sell the farm and those forty acres of fences. Although it was financially necessary, it brought me much sadness, but a legacy isn't always monetary. When I left my father lying on his hospital bed knowing it would be his last hours or days on earth, he wasn't thinking about himself. His final words to me before I left to go back home that day due to my husband's condition was, "I hope everything will be ok". Those words struck my heart like a dagger. No matter what he was going through and his life was being held in the balance between life and death, he thought of me and those I love; specifically my husband who was also laying on a hospital bed in California. At that moment, he was leaving me his legacy of how a loving and caring parent should be.

Both a legacy and inheritance are in some ways quite similar. Both can be handed down to others. A person can inherit money, property as well as character and beliefs. A legacy can also be handed down, either by a will or example. My father's legacy wasn't a monetary one. It was really a spiritual one. He didn't have much money to hand down to his children but he certainly handed down very strong morals, appreciation for hard work, and respect for ourselves, our parents and others, and a love for the Lord. That kind of legacy means more to me than if he had millions of dollars to give me to place in my hope chest. I'm eternally grateful for that.

Our Heavenly Father leaves us a legacy too. If we believe in the One who He has sent into the world to pay a debt He didn't owe because we owed a debt we couldn't pay, we will have an eternal legacy. God's Word promises us this in Ephesians 1:11-13 *"And you also were included in Christ when you heard the word of truth, the gospel of your salvation. Having believed, you are marked in Him with a seal, the promised Holy Spirit, who is a deposit guaranteeing our inheritance until the redemption of those who are God's possession-to the praise of His Glory."* Also, Titus 3:4-7 says *"But when the kindness and love of God our Savior appeared, He saved us, not because of righteous things we had done, but because of His mercy. He saved us through the washing of rebirth and renewal by the Holy Spirit, whom He poured out on us generously through Jesus Christ our Savior, so that, having been justified by His grace, we might become heirs having the hope of eternal life."*

Not only will this legacy include eternal life with Him in Heaven, but it will provide us hope and peace while we are still living in a sinful world. While we wait, He left us the Holy Spirit to be our guide and our light in a dark world. The Spirit teaches us the truths of God's Word and keeps us on that narrow road. The Spirit is a lamp and a light to my path and whispers "go this way or that" and sometimes "don't go at all" or "Be still and know that I am God".

In the light of everything in this book, I have to ask the question. What kind of legacy will I leave my loved ones and friends? What kind of legacy will you leave? Will it be a legacy of bitterness, hatred, prejudice, judgment, pride or an unforgiving spirit? Or will it be a legacy of love, mercy, forgiveness or peace? Words and actions can hurt or heal. They can have a negative or positive impact. They can crush a spirit or lift a spirit. They can pull others in your life away from God or towards God.

Galatians 2:20 says, *"I have been crucified with Christ and I no longer live, But Christ lives in me. The life I now live in the body, I live by faith in the Son of God, who loved me and gave himself for me."* The Holy Spirit lives in us and continually sanctifies us in order to live according to God's Word. In Paul's letter to the Colossians, he prayed with encouragement for them to live worthy of the Lord and please Him in every way, bearing fruit in every good work, and grow in the knowledge of God, so that they have great endurance, patience, and joyfully giving thanks to the Father, who has qualified them to share in the inheritance of the saints. This should also be our prayer for the sake of ourselves and for the sake of our legacy.

What kind of fences will you build and continue to mend as you go through life here on earth?

Let's again look at the Fruits of the Spirit:

- *Love*
- *Peace*
- *Patience*
- *Kindness*
- *Goodness*
- *Faithfulness*
- *Gentleness*
- *Self-control*

Paul again spoke of that kind of legacy in his prayer to the Ephesians in Ephesians 3:16-19 *"I pray that out of His glorious riches he may strengthen you with power through His Spirit in your inner being, so that Christ may dwell in your hearts through faith. And I pray that you, being rooted and established in love, may have power, together with all the saints, to grasp how wide and long and high and deep is the love of Christ, and to know this love that surpasses knowledge—that you may be filled to the measure of all the fullness of God."*

As I mentioned before, my dad was a very kind, loving and considerate man and father. On the farm, we had an old popcorn popper, which had a lid with a spinner connected. Once the popcorn would heat up on the stove, we would turn the spinner until the popcorn was all popped. If we left it on the stove too long, it would burn. I got so excited for the first time I got to pop it myself; and wouldn't you know, I left it on the burner too long and it burned. I was so disappointed because I wanted it to be good and that my family would like it. I'm sure everyone saw the disappointment on my face; especially my dad. My dad, in the most loving and kind way, scooped up some burned popcorn into his dish, took a bite and said it was good. I knew it wasn't but he made me feel better about a bad situation.

On the farm, we had lots of fried chicken for dinner (also known as supper in the Midwest). For years, I really thought my dad's favorite pieces of the chicken was the wing or back. Looking back I came to realize that wasn't really the case. He wanted to make sure his family got the bigger pieces before he picked his. Once he saw that everyone picked what pieces they wanted, the only pieces left were the wings and the back. My dad sacrificed his favorite pieces to make sure his family had what they wanted. God does the same thing for His children. He sacrificed everything so we can have life and have it more abundantly. He accepts and loves us just as we are. That's grace!

Even many years after his death, my father's words still linger, "If you don't have anything nice to say, don't say anything at all", and "Don't fight; get along". My earthly father's legacy continues on, even in generations to come through the life that he lived and the words he said. His example fully exhibited the Heavenly Father's attributes.

So as I continue my journey of faith and wait for God's lesson to begin again, I will keep walking in His wonderful fences of Grace, whether I pass the next test or not. One day when I cross over that eternal chasm from mortal to immortal and I reach that building not made with hands within the eternal fences of Heaven, I will be met by my Heavenly Father and be reunited with my earthly father. Both have given me a legacy that will last forever. My prayer is that not only I, but that you too will leave a legacy that would reach far beyond this life into the eternal.

Dad, you are greatly loved and missed. Can't wait to see you again!

A FATHER'S LEGACY

My father was a gentle man;

A quiet soul was he.

He loved the Lord with all his heart

And loved his family.

Human, as he truly was;

A saint, was he to me.

He lived his life, poor some would say;

But I would not agree.

My father was a child of the King;

An heir to royalty.

He lived for God, but in death he left

A father's legacy.

For I was blessed to have had

A father, full of love.

He was a true reflection

Of the Father up above.

His arms of grace and mercy;

An example to me here

Of my Heavenly Father's countenance;

It was seen so very clear.

Although he's gone, he did not die;

But living still through me.

He lived for God, but in death he left

A father's legacy.

@Catherine Garrett – June 2002

CHAPTER TEN

OPEN FENCES OF FAITH AND GRACE
(GOD'S WORD IN ACTION)

Okay, okay God! I get it! Of course, I get it; at least until He gives me the next lesson of faith around the next corner of life. And, why is that? Why do I continue to have to learn over and over this lesson of faith? Why don't I trust God in every circumstance of life? Why can't I always see God working in the circumstance? Why isn't my faith strong enough day by day and step by step? I'm sure you've asked these same questions too. But the only answer I can come up with is……..wait for it……….

……..because we're human!

Please don't let that discourage you. I've got some good news of grace! Remember, God is omniscient. He knows exactly when our faith will be strong enough, when we will lack the faith we need and when we will fall right on our faces when our faith is smaller than a mustard seed. The good news is that God is also merciful and full of grace. In fact, He is abounding in mercy and grace. The word abounding doesn't provide just the right amount, but God is overflowing with mercy and grace. He is plentiful beyond measure to provide all we need, whether it's tangible or spiritual. But there's more good news. He never runs out! His mercy, grace and provision are always fully supplied and accessible to his children; even when we don't ask for them or deserve them. King David wrote about

God's mercy in Psalm 25:6 *"Remember, O Lord, your great mercy and love, for they are from old. Remember not the sins of my youth and my rebellious ways; according to your love remember me, for you are good, O Lord."* Because we are human, we are sinners. But God, in His great love and mercy forgives us and continues to sanctify us so that we learn and grow to be like Christ while here on this planet. That's why God never gives up on us.

    Grace cancels out human merit. We're not strong enough to do what God wants us to do (or not do) without His power. I recall a time on the farm when we were experiencing a very strong summer storm. It was getting close to milking time when all of a sudden the storm caused the lights to go out. Living on a farm most of his life, my dad certainly knew how to milk a cow by hand, but it certainly saved him a great deal of time when he could use electric milking machines. He knew that by plugging into the power of that electricity, his job would be a lot easier. But that power wasn't available because of the storm so my dad, mom, my sisters and I, with flashlights in hand, headed for the barn. All at once lightning struck one of the metal roofed silos which sat right behind the barn. I must have jumped ten feet off of the ground. My sisters and I took off running full speed like we were being chased by a herd of buffalo. After catching my breath, I remember peeking out the barn door to see my mom and dad, who seemed unaffected by what had just happened, walking slowly and calmly toward the barn. Perhaps they knew that God was in control and His power was stronger than their fear. Just like the electrical power that helped my dad's milking job easier, plugging into God's power makes our lives easier; especially when it comes to faith in the face of uncertainty. It replenishes us when our faith loses power all together.

Faith is God's Word in action. Faith, like many other actions, is a choice. We have faith that when we turn on the light switch, the light will come on. We have faith in the chair we're about ready it sit on will hold us. We have faith that when we turn the key in the car that it will start. So why is it so difficult to have faith in God's plan, even though we can't see it? Because, like Thomas, it's easier to trust in things we can see rather than things we can't see. Tangible vs. the invisible. Physical and touchable vs. the spiritual and supernatural. We can choose to look at the circumstances or we can choose to look to God. Many scriptures tell us to walk by faith. Paul says in Romans 1:17b *"The righteous will live by faith"*. Paul also says in 2 Corinthians 5:7 *"We live by faith, not by sight."* In Paul's letter to the Ephesians, he says "Ephesians 6:16 *"Take up the shield of faith, with which you can extinguish all the flaming arrows of the evil one."* And finally Jesus says in Mark 9:23 *"Everything is possible for him who believes."*

Hebrews 11 is considered to be the "Hall of Faith" of the Bible. For our encouragement, it outlines some examples of faith of Biblical Patriarchs. It starts out with the very familiar verse which says *"Faith is sure of what we hoped for and certain of what we do not see."* As I've mentioned before, this verse needs to be tattooed on my forehead. Chapter 11 continues on to tell us about those individuals who God is commending for their faith.

BY FAITH......

- Abel offered God a better sacrifice than Cain because of his righteousness
- Enoch, because he pleased God, God took him and didn't experience death
- Noah became heir of righteousness because he built an ark to save his family when God warned him about things not yet seen
- Abraham, even though he didn't know where he was going, obeyed God to go to a place he would later receive as his inheritance
- Abraham, even though he was past age and Sarah herself was barren, believed God who promised that his descendants would be as numerous as the stars
- Abraham, when God tested him, offered Isaac as a sacrifice in obedience to God's command; as a result received the promise of many descendants through his offspring
- Isaac blessed Jacob and Esau in regard to their future
- Jacob, when he was dying, blessed each of Joseph's sons.
- Joseph, when his end was near, spoke about the exodus of the Israelites from Egypt, even though it hadn't happened yet
- Moses; parents hid him for three months after he was born to protect him from being killed
- Moses, choosing to be mistreated along with the people of God rather than enjoy the pleasures of sin

for a short time; left Egypt, not fearing the king's anger, was persevered by God because he saw Him who is invisible
- Moses by keeping the Passover and sprinkling of blood, so that the destroyer of the firstborn would not touch the firstborn of Israel
- The people passed through the Red Sea on dry land while the Egyptians who followed them were drowned
- The walls of Jericho fell, after the people had marched around them for seven days in obedience to God's commands
- The prostitute Rahab, because she helped the Israelite spies, she was not killed with those who were disobedient

The rest of the chapter goes on and on with many other faithful heroes of faith. Will you be among those who live by faith and stand up against all odds like those in the book of Hebrews? Will I?

So what does God's Grace have to do with faith? Everything! It starts and ends with Grace. By Grace we are saved through our faith in Jesus Christ for our salvation. Even while we were still sinners, Christ died for us. It is a gift and can't be earned. Faith in action is our response to Grace. Despite our imperfections and failing human efforts, God saves us and preserves us by His Grace alone.

When I was young, I started out with training wheels on my bicycle until I felt confident enough to ride with balance. Our journey of faith is the same. Our lessons of faith start out really small and as the years go by, each new lesson requires greater faith. As each lesson becomes harder and harder, God's Grace becomes more and more visible. God helps us out. When we become believers, God doesn't expect us to be able to split the Red Sea or walk on water immediately. He starts us with small baby steps of faith. He goes slowly and gives us a chance to catch up. That's grace. The more He tests our faith, the more we rely on Him and His grace to help us in the next situation we face.

In Hebrews 12:2, Paul wrote that Jesus is the author and finisher of our faith. He is the beginning, perfecter and rewarder of it. Everything, including faith, begins and ends with Jesus. The scripture says, *"Let us fix our eyes on Jesus, the author and finisher of our faith, who for the joy set before Him endured the cross, scorning its shame, and sat down at the right hand of the throne of God."* He preceded our faith when He obeyed the Father and endured the cross. He purchased our faith for us. He also fulfilled it on our behalf. He is the finisher of our faith and his work of faith brought power to the souls of His people. His grace helps us get across the finish line where we'll see Him face to face.

The definition of the word faith is being confident in and trust God and His Word to be true. The definition of the word faithful is that God is consistent in His Word. This is seen in II Samuel 22:31 which says, "As for God, His way is perfect; the Word of God is flawless. What He says, He will do.

So, how do we obtain faith? Romans 10:17 says *"Faith comes by hearing and hearing by the Word of God."* As we go through our lessons of faith, the Holy Spirit teaches us through God's Word. The Bible just isn't just another book on the shelf. The words come straight from God's mouth to our ears. II Timothy 3:16 says, *"All Scripture is God-breathed and is useful for teaching, rebuking, correcting and training in righteousness, so that the man of God may be thoroughly equipped for every good work."* Hebrews 4:12 tells us that God's Word is living and active. God has given us many scriptures to teach us what faith is in order to equip us in our life's journey. First we have to learn it; then effectively use it.

Standing on all of God's promises and our faith in Him alone is without a doubt, necessary in this world of chaos and insecurities. These are our responses to God's unmeasurable Grace. Grace in our doubts. Grace in our discouragement. Grace in our missteps. Grace in our disobedience. Grace in our weakness. Grace in our humanness. Grace in God's direction of our life's journey even when we want to go another direction. Grace when he sends rain in the midst of drought and hopelessness. Grace through His provision of an overabundance of Blue Lake green beans in a garden full of grasshoppers. Grace in the healing of a gunshot wound. Grace even in the face of death.

Over and over, I have discovered that in all lessons of faith, God's faithfulness outweighed my weak faith. God's faithfulness and our faith works together to fulfill His perfect purpose in our lives. In every walk of life and circumstance, whether rich or poor, young or old, God's purpose remains the same. He loves His children and always wants the best for them. Jeremiah 29:11 says *"For I know the plans I have for you, declares the Lord, plans to prosper you and not to harm you (grace), plans to give you a hope and a future. (Legacy/inheritance)."*

Despite how many hardships the Apostle Paul experienced, he spoke with an eternal perspective in Philippians 3:7-9 when he said *"But whatever was to my profit I now consider loss for the sake of Christ. What is more, I consider everything a loss compared to the surpassing greatness of knowing Christ Jesus my Lord, for whose sake I have lost all things. I consider them rubbish that I may gain Christ and be found in Him, not having a righteousness of my own but that which is through faith in Christ--the righteousness that comes from God and is by faith."*

Just as the farm fences represented many things in my life, God's fences represent many things in a Christian's life. God has built fences for our protection, His providence, our security in Him, faith through life's challenges, His power and mighty works, light for our journey, provision for our needs, peace and hope even in despair, nourishment in times of thirst and life eternal in the face of death. We still serve a God who creates, provides all we need, heals, gives peace in our struggles, protection in our journey and the power of His Spirit throughout our earthly journey.

The many lessons I learned while living on my forty-acre farm in Kansas have remained in my heart and will continue to do so until God calls me "Home" to be with Him. I was surrounded with fences on the farm but I have been surrounded by God's fences throughout my entire life, which has a much greater eternal value. By staying in God's Light and Word, walking in His footsteps and not getting off onto my own path, has resulted in God's security and peace in my journey. When we all do this, we also become closer to God through His Word, and in turn, our faith in Him increases.

He also taught me that God's fences of protection, providence, grace and love will always provide in ways beyond my imagination. By believing God will walk hand-in-hand with me; even in the face of death, has given me a better understanding of who God is and how to trust Him in everything. The closer walk I have with Jesus, the more of what this world offers diminishes and the more "Homesick" I become. But while I wait for that glorious day................

........His lesson of faith continues.

Now faith is being sure of what we hope for and certain of what we do not see.

Hebrews 11:1

Made in the USA
San Bernardino, CA
11 July 2020